HISTORIC HIGHWAYS OF AMERICA

VOLUME 4

BRADDOCK'S GRAVE

[The depression on the right is the ancient track of Braddock's Road; near the single cluster of gnarled apple trees in the meadow beyond, Braddock died and was first buried]

HISTORIC HIGHWAYS OF AMERICA
VOLUME 4

Braddock's Road

AND

THREE RELATIVE PAPERS

BY

ARCHER BUTLER HULBERT

With Maps and Illustrations

AMS PRESS
NEW YORK

Reprinted from the edition of 1902-05, Cleveland
First AMS EDITION published 1971
Manufactured in the United States of America

International Standard Book Number:
COMPLETE SET   0-404-03420-9
Volume Four   0-404-03424-1

Library of Congress Number: 70-147112

AMS PRESS INC.
NEW YORK, N.Y. 10003

CONTENTS

ILLUSTRATIONS

PREFACE

THE French were invariably defeated by the British on this continent because the latter overcame natural obstacles which the former blindly trusted as insurmountable. The French made a league with the Alleghenies — and Washington and Braddock and Forbes conquered the Alleghenies; the French, later, blindly trusted the crags at Louisbourg and Quebec — and the dauntless Wolfe, in both instances, accomplished the seemingly impossible.

The building of Braddock's Road in 1755 across the Alleghenies was the first significant token in the West of the British grit which finally overcame. Few roads ever cost so much, ever amounted to so little at first, and then finally played so important a part in the development of any continent.

A. B. H.

MARIETTA, O., December 8, 1902.

Braddock's Road

and

Three Relative Papers

CHAPTER I

IF Providence had reversed the decree which allowed Frenchmen to settle the St. Lawrence and Englishmen the middle Atlantic seaboard, and, instead, had brought Englishmen to Quebec and Frenchmen to Jamestown, it is sure that the English conquest of the American continent would not have cost the time and blood it did.

The Appalachian mountain system proved a tremendous handicap to Saxon conquest. True, there were waterways inland, the Connecticut, Hudson, Delaware, James, and Potomac rivers, but these led straight into the mountains where for generations the feeble settlements could not spread and where explorers became disheartened ere the rich empire beyond was ever reached.

The St. Lawrence, on the other hand,

offered a rough but sure course tempting
ambitious men onward to the great lake
system from which it flowed, and the Otta-
wa River offered yet another course to the
same splendid goal. So, while the stolid
English were planting sure feet along the
seaboard, New France was spreading by
leaps and bounds across the longitudes. But,
wide-spread as these discoveries were, they
were discoveries only — the feet of those
who should occupy and defend the land
discovered were heavy where the light
paddle of the voyageur had glistened
brightly beneath the noon-day sun. It was
one thing to seek out such an empire and
quite another thing to occupy and fortify it.
The French reached the Mississippi at the
beginning of the last quarter of the seven-
teenth century; ten years after the middle
of the eighteenth they lost all the territory
between the Atlantic and Mississippi —
though during the last ten years of their
possession they had attempted heroically
to take the nine stitches where a genera-
tion before the proverbial one stitch would
have been of twenty-fold more advantage.
The transportation of arms and stores up-

stream into the interior, around the foaming rapids and thundering falls that impeded the way, was painfully arduous labor, and the inspiration of the swift explorers, flushed with fevered dreams, was lacking to the heavy trains which toiled so far in the rear.

There were three points at which the two nations, France and England, met and struck fire in the interior of North America, and in each instance it was the French who were the aggressors — because of the easy means of access which they had into the disputed frontier region. They came up the Chaudière and down the Kennebec or up the Richelieu and Lake Champlain, striking at the heart of New England; they ascended the St. Lawrence and entered Lake Ontario, coveted and claimed by the Province of New York; they pushed through Lake Ontario and down the Allegheny to the Ohio River, which Virginia loved and sought to guard. The French tried to guard these three avenues of approach by erecting fortresses on the Richelieu River, on Lakes Champlain, Ontario, and Erie, and on the Allegheny and Ohio Rivers. These forts were the weights on the net which the French were stretching from the mouth of the St. Lawrence to the mouth of the Mississippi. And when that net was drawn taut New England and New York and Virginia would be swept into the sea!

It was a splendid scheme — but the weights were not heavy enough. After interminable blunders and delays the English broke into the net and then by desperate floundering tore it to fragments. They reached the line of forts by three routes, each difficult and hazardous, for in any case vast stretches of forests were to be passed; and until the very last, the French had strong Indian allies who guarded these forests with valor worthy of a happier cause. New England defended herself by ascending the Hudson and crossing the portage to Lake George and Lake Champlain. New York ascended the Mohawk and, crossing the famous Oneida portage to Odeida Lake, descended the Onondaga River to Oswego on Lake Ontario. Virginia spreading out, according to her unchallenged claims, across the entire continent,

could only reach the French on the Ohio by
ascending the Potomac to a point near the
mouth of Wills Creek, whence an Indian
path led northwestward over a hundred
miles to the Monongahela, which was
descended to its junction with the Ohio.
The two former routes, to Lake Champlain
and to Lake Ontario, were, with short portages, practically all-water routes, over
which provisions and army stores could be
transported northward to the zone into
which the French had likewise come by
water-routes. The critical points of both
routes of both hostile nations were the
strategic portages where land travel was
rendered imperative by the difficulties
of navigation. On these portages many
forts instantly sprang into existence — in
some instances mere posts and entrepôts, in
some cases strongly fortified citadels.

The route from Virginia to the Ohio
Valley, finally made historic by the English General Braddock, was by far the
most difficult of all the ways by which the
English could meet the French. The Potomac was navigable for small boats at favorable seasons for varying distances; but

beyond the mountains the first water reached, the Youghiogheny, was useless for military purposes, as Washington discovered during the march of the Virginia Regiment, 1754. The route had, however, been marked out under the direction of Captain Thomas Cresap, for the Ohio Company, and was, at the time of Washington's expedition, the most accessible passageway from Virginia to the " Forks of the Ohio." The only other Virginian thoroughfare westward brought the traveller around into the valley of the Great Kanawha which empties into the Ohio two hundred odd miles below the junction of the Allegheny and Monongahela rivers. It was over this slight trail by Wills Creek, Great Meadows, and the Forks of the Ohio that Washington had gone in 1753 to the French forts on French Creek; and it was this path that the same undaunted youth widened, the year after, in order to haul his swivels westward with the vanguard of Colonel Fry's army which was to drive the French from the Ohio. Washington's Road — as Nemacolin's Path should, in all conscience, be known — was widened to the

summit of Mount Braddock. From Mount
Braddock Washington's little force retraced
their steps over the road they had built in
the face of the larger French army sent
against them until they were driven to bay
in their little fortified camp, Fort Necessity, in Great Meadows, where the capitulation took place after an all-day's battle.
Marching out with the honors of war, the
remnant of this first English army crawled
painfully back to Wills Creek. All this
took place in the summer of 1754.

The inglorious campaign ending thus in
dismay was of considerably more moment
than its dejected survivors could possibly
have imagined. Small as were the numbers
of contestants on both sides, and distant
though the scene of conflict might have
been, the peace between England and
France was at this moment poised too deli-
cately not to be disturbed by even the
faintest roll of musketry in the distant
unknown Alleghenies.

Washington had been able neither to
fight successfully nor to avoid a battle by
conducting a decent retreat because the
reinforcements expected from Virginia

were not sent him. These "reinforcements" were Rutherford's and Clarke's
Independent Companies of Foot which
Governor Dinwiddie had ordered from New
York to Virginia but which did not arrive
in Hampton Roads until the eighth of
June. On the first of September these
troops were marched to Wills Creek, where,
being joined by Captain Demerie's Independent Company from South Carolina,
they began, on the twelfth of September,
the erection of a fort. The building of this
fort by Virginia nearly a hundred miles west
of Winchester (then a frontier post) is only
paralleled by the energy of Massachusetts in
building two forts in the same year on the
Kennebec River — Fort Western and Fort
Halifax. New York had almost forgotten
her frontier forts at Saratoga and Oswego,
and the important portage between the
Hudson and Lake George was undefended
while the French were building both Fort
Ticonderoga and Fort Frederick (Crown
Point) on Lake Champlain. New York and
New England could have seized and fortified Lake Champlain prior to French
encroachment as easily as Virginia could

fortify Wills Creek.   Virginia, however, had been assisted from the royal chest, while the assemblies of the other colonies were in the customary state of turmoil, governor against legislature.   The intermediate province of Pennsylvania, home of the peaceful Quakers, looked askance upon the darkening war-clouds and had done little or nothing for the protection of her populous frontiers.   As a result, therefore, the Virginian route to the French, though longest and most difficult, was made, by the erection of Fort Cumberland at Wills Creek, at once the most conspicuous.

Fort Cumberland, named in honor of the Duke of Cumberland, Captain-general of the English Army, was located on an eminence between Wills Creek and the Potomac, two hundred yards from the former and about four hundred yards from the latter.   Its length was approximately two hundred yards and its breadth nearly fifty yards; and " is built," writes an eye-witness in 1755, " by logs driven into the ground, and about 12 feet above it, with embrasures for 12 guns, and 10 mounted 4 pounders, besides stocks for swivels, and loop holes for small arms." As the accompanying map indicates, the fort was built with a view to the protection of the storehouses erected at the mouth of Wills Creek by the Ohio Company. This is another suggestion of the close connection between the commercial and military expansion of Virginia into the Ohio basin. Wherever a storehouse of the Ohio Company was erected a fort soon followed — with the exception of the strategic position at the junction of the Allegheny and Monongahela where English fort building was brought to a sudden end by the arrival of the French, who, on English beginnings, erected Fort Duquesne in 1754. A little fort at the mouth of Redstone Creek on the Monongahela had been erected in 1753 but that, together with the blasted remains of Fort Necessity, fell into the hands of the French in the campaign of 1754. Consequently, at the dawning of the memorable year 1755, Fort Cumberland was the most advanced English position in the West. The French Indian allies saw to it that it was safe for no Englishman to step even one pace nearer the Ohio; they skulked

continually in the neighboring forests and committed many depredations almost within range of the guns of Fort Cumberland.

CHAPTER II

THE VIRGINIA CAMPAIGN

GOVERNOR DINWIDDIE'S zeal had increased in inverse ratio to the success of Virginian arms. After Washington's repulse at Fort Necessity he redoubled his energies, incited by a letter received from one of Washington's hostages at Fort Duquesne. Colonel Innes was appointed to command the Virginia troops and superintend the erection of Fort Cumberland, while Washington was ordered to fill up his depleted companies by enlistments and to move out again to Fort Cumberland. Indeed it was only by objections urged in the very strongest manner that the inconsiderate Governor was deterred from launching another destitute and ill-equipped expedition into the snow-drifted Alleghenies.

But there was activity elsewhere than in Virginia during the winter of 1754–5.

Contrecœur, commanding at Fort Duquesne, sent clear reports of the campaign
of 1754. The French cause was strength-
ening. The success of the French had had
a wonderful effect on the indifferent Indians; hundreds before only half-hearted
came readily under French domination.
All this was of utmost moment to New
France, possibly of more importance than
keeping her chain of forts to Quebec un-
broken. As Joncaire, the drunken commander on the Allegheny, had told Washington in 1753, the English could raise two
men in America to their one — but not
including their Indians.

It is, probably, impossible for us to re-
alize with what feelings the French antic-
ipated war with England on the American
continent. The long campaigns in Europe
had cost both nations much and had
brought no return to either. Even Mar-
shal Saxe's brilliant victories were pur-
chased at a fabulous price, and, at the end,
Louis had given up all that was gained in
order to pose " as a Prince and not as a
merchant." But in America there was a
prize which both of these nations desired

and which was worth fighting for — the grandest prize ever won in war! Between the French and English colonies lay this black forest stretching from Maine through New York and Pennsylvania and Virginia to the Gulf of Mexico. It seemed, to the French, the silliest dream imaginable for the English to plan to pierce this forest and conquer New France. To reach any of the French forts a long passage by half-known courses through an inhospitable wilderness was necessary; and the French knew by a century of experience what a Herculean task it was to carry troops and stores over the inland water and land ways of primeval America. But for the task they had had much assistance from the Indians and were favored in many instances by the currents of these rivers; the English had almost no Indian allies and in every case were compelled to ascend their rivers to reach the French. However, the formation of the Ohio Company and the lively days of the summer of 1754 in the Alleghenies aroused France as nothing else could; here was one young Virginian officer who had found his way through the forests, and there was no telling how many more there might be like him. And France, tenfold more disturbed by Washington's campaign than there was need for, performed wonders during the winter of 1754–5. The story of the action at Fort Necessity was transmitted to London and was represented by the British ambassadors at Paris as an open violation of the peace, " which did not meet with the same degree of respect," writes a caustic historian, " as on former occasions of complaint: the time now nearly approaching for the French to pull off the mask of moderation and peace." [1] As if to confirm this suspicion, the French marine became suddenly active, the Ministry ordered a powerful armament to be fitted at Brest; " in all these armaments," wrote the Earl of Holderness's secret agent, " there appeared a plain design to make settlements and to build forts; besides, that it was given out, they resolved to augment the fortifications at Louisburg, and to build more forts on the Ohio." [2]

But there was activity now in England,

[1] Entick, *History of the Late War*, vol. i., p. 110.
[2] *Id.*, vol. i., p. 124.

too. Governor Sharpe of Maryland, but lately appointed Commander-in-chief in America, had only a hint of what was being planned and was to have even less share in its accomplishment; in vain his friends extolled him as honest — "a little less honesty," declared George II, characteristically, "and a little more ability were more to be desired at the moment." And the rule worked on both sides of the Atlantic. American affairs had long been in the hands of the Secretary of the Board of Trade, the Duke of Newcastle, as perfect an ass as ever held high office. He had opposed every policy that did not accord with his own "time serving selfishness" with a persistency only matched by his unparalleled ignorance. Once thrown into a panic, it is said, at a rumor that a large French army had been thrown into Cape Breton, he was asked where the necessary transports had been secured.

"Transports," he shrieked, "I tell you they marched by land!"

"By land, to the island of Cape Breton?" was the astonished reply.

"What, is Cape Breton an island? Are

you sure of that?" and he ran away with an " Egad, I will go directly and tell the King that Cape Breton is an island!" It is not surprising that a government which could ever have tolerated such a man in high office should have neglected, then abused, and then lost its American colonies.

But Newcastle gave way to an abler man. The new campaign in North America was the conception of the Captain-general of the British Army, the Duke of Cumberland, hero of Culloden.

On November 14, 1754, King George opened Parliament with the statement that " His principal view should be to strengthen the foundation, and secure the duration of a general peace; to improve the present advantages of it for promoting the trade of his good subjects, and protecting those possessions which constitute one great source of their wealth and commerce." Only in this vague way did His Majesty refer to the situation in America, lest he precipitate a debate; but Parliament took the cue and voted over four million pounds — one million of which was to be devoted to augmen ing England's forces " by land

and sea." Cumberland's plan for the operations against the French in America had, sometime before, been forwarded to the point of selecting a Generalissimo to be sent to that continent. Major-General Edward Braddock was appointed to the service, upon the Duke of Cumberland's recommendation, on September 24.

Edward Braddock was a lieutenant-colonel of the line and a major of the Foot Guards, the choicest corps of the British army — a position which cost the holder no less than eighteen thousand dollars. He was born in Ireland but was not Irish, for neither Scot, Irish, nor Papist could aspire to the meanest rank of the Foot Guards. He was as old as his century. His promotion in the army had been jointly due to the good name of his father, Edward Braddock I, who was retired as Major-general in 1715, to his passion for strict discipline, and to the favor of His Grace the Duke of Cumberland. Braddock's personal bravery was proverbial; it was said that his troops never faced a danger when their commander was not "greedy to lead." In private life he was dissolute; in disposition,

" a very Iroquois," according to Walpole. Yet certain of his friends denied the brutality which many attributed to him. " As we were walking in the Park," one of Braddock's admirers has recorded, " we heard a poor fellow was to be chastized; when I requested the General to beg off the offender. Upon his application to the general officer, whose name was Dury, he asked Braddock, How long since he had divested himself of brutality and the insolence of his manner? To which the other replied, ' You never knew me insolent to my inferiors. It is only to such rude men as yourself that I behave with the spirit which I think they deserve.' " [3] And yet, when his sister Fanny hanged herself with a silver girdle to her chamber door, after losing her fortune at the gaming tables, the brute of a brother observed, " I always thought she would play till she would be forced to tuck herself up." On the other hand it need not be forgotten that Braddock was for forty-three years in the service of the famed Coldstream Guards; that he

[3] *Apology for the Life of George Anne Bellamy*, vol. iii., p. 55.

probably conducted himself with courage in the Vigo expedition and in the Low Countries, and was a survivor of bloody Dettingen, Culloden, Fontenoy, and Bergen-op-Zoom.   In 1753 he was stationed at Gibraltar where, " with all his brutality," writes Walpole, " he made himself adored, and where scarce any governor was endured before." [4]

Two months and one day after Braddock's commission was signed he received two letters of instructions, one from the King and one from the Duke of Cumberland. " For your better direction in discharge of ye Trust thereby reposed in You," reads the King's letter, " We have judged it proper to give You the following Instructions."   The document is divided into thirteen heads:

1.   Two regiments of Foot commanded by Sir Peter Halket and Colonel Dunbar, with a train of artillery and necessary ships were ordered to " repair to North America."

2.   Braddock ordered to proceed to America and take under his command these

<hr />

[4] *Letters of Walpole*, (edited by Cunningham, London 1877), vol. ii., p. 461.

troops, cultivating meanwhile "a good understanding & correspondence with Aug. Keppel Esqr." who was appointed commander of the American squadron.

3.   Orders him also to take command of and properly distribute 3000 men which the Governors of the provinces had been ordered to raise to serve under Governor Shirley and Sir William Pepperell; informs him that Sir John St. Clair, deputy Quarter Master General, and Jas. Pitcher Esqr., " our commissary of ye musters, in North America," had been sent to prepare for the arrival of the troops from Ireland and for raising the troops in America.   Upon Braddock's arrival he should inform himself of the progress of these preparations.

4.   Provisions for the troops from Ireland had been prepared lest, upon arrival in America, they should be in want.

5.   " Whereas, We have given Orders to our said Gov^{rs} to provide carefully a sufficient Quantity of fresh victuals for ye use of our Troops at their arrival, & y^t they should also furnish all our officers who may have occasion to go from Place to Place, with all necessaries for travelling by Land,

in case there are no means of going by
Sea; & likewise, to observe and obey all
such orders as shall be given by You or Per-
sons appointed by you from time to time
for quartering Troops, impressing Carriages, & providing all necessaries for such
Forces as shall arrive or be raised in America, and y^t the s^d several Services shall be
performed at the charge of ye respective
Governments, wherein the same shall happen. It is our Will & Pleasure y^t you
should, pursuant thereto, apply to our s^d
Governors, or any of them, upon all such
Exigencies.''

6. The Governors had been directed
'' to endeavor to prevail upon ye Assemblies
of their respective Provinces to raise forth-
with as large a sum as can be afforded as
their contribution to a common Fund, to
be employed provisionally for ye general
Service in North America.'' Braddock
was urged to assist in this and have great
care as to its expenditure.

7. Concerns Braddock's relations with
the colonial governors; especially directing
that a Council of War which shall include
them be formed to determine, by majority

vote, matters upon which no course has been defined.

8. " You will not only cultivate ye best Harmony & Friendship possible with ye several Governors of our Colonies & Provinces, but likewise with ye Chiefs of ye Indian Tribes . . to endeavor to engage them to take part & act with our Forces, in such operations as you shall think most expedient."

9. Concerns securing the alliance and interest of the Indians and giving them presents.

10. Orders Braddock to prevent any commerce between the French and the English provinces.

11. Concerning the relative precedency of royal and colonial commissions.

12. Describes the copies of documents enclosed to Braddock concerning previous relations with the colonies for defense against French encroachment; " . . And as Extracts of Lieut Govr Dinwiddie's Letters of May 10th, June 18th, & July 24th, relating to the Summons of the Fort which was erecting on ye Forks of ye Monongahela, and ye Skirmish y^t followed soon after, &

likewise of ye action in the Great Meadows, near the River Ohio, are herewith delivered to you, you will be fully acquainted with what has hitherto happened of a hostile Nature upon the Banks of that River.''

13. Concerns future correspondence between Braddock and the Secretaries of State to whom his reports were to be sent.

The communication from the Duke of Cumberland written by his Aide, Colonel Napier, throws much light upon the verbal directions which Braddock received before he sailed:

'' His Royal Highness the Duke, in the several audiences he has given you, entered into a particular explanation of every part of the service you are about to be employed in; and as a better rule for the execution of His Majesty's instructions, he last Saturday communicated to you his own sentiments of this affair, and since you were desirous of forgetting no part thereof, he has ordered me to deliver them to you in writing. His Royal Highness has this service very much at heart, as it is of the highest importance to his majesty's American dominions, and to the honour of his troops employed in those parts. His Royal Highness likewise takes a particular interest in it, as it concerns you, whom he recommended to his majesty to be nominated to the chief command.

" His Royal Highness's opinion is, that immediately after your landing, you consider what artillery and other implements of war it will be necessary to transport to Will's Creek for your first operation on the Ohio, that it may not fail you in the service; and that you form a second field train, with good officers and soldiers, which shall be sent to Albany and be ready to march for the second operation at Niagara. You are to take under your command as many as you think necessary of the two companies of artillery that are in Nova Scotia and Newfoundland as soon as the season will allow, taking care to leave enough to defend the Island. Captain Ord, a very experienced officer, of whom his Royal Highness has a great opinion, will join you as soon as possible.

" As soon as Shirley's and Pepperel's regiments are near complete, his Royal

Highness is of opinion you should cause them to encamp, not only that they may sooner be disciplined, but also to draw the attention of the French and keep them in suspense about the place you really design to attack. His Royal Highness does not doubt that the officers and captains of the several companies will answer his expectation in forming and disciplining their respective troops. The most strict discipline is always necessary, but more particularly so in the service you are engaged in. Wherefore his Royal Highness recommends to you that it be constantly observed among the troops under your command, and to be particularly careful that they be not thrown into a panic by the Indians, with whom they are yet unacquainted, whom the French will certainly employ to frighten them. His Royal Highness recommends to you the visiting your posts night and day; that your Colonels and other officers be careful to do it; and that you yourself frequently set them the example; and give all your troops plainly to understand that no excuse will be admitted for any surprise whatsoever.

VIEW OF FORT CUMBERLAND IN 1755

" Should the Ohio expedition continue any considerable time, and Pepperell's and Shirley's regiments be found sufficient to undertake in the mean while the reduction of Niagara, his Royal Highness would have you consider whether you could go there in person, leaving the command of the troops on the Ohio to some officer on whom you might depend, unless you shall think it better for the service to send to those troops some person whom you had designed to command on the Ohio; but this is a nice affair, and claims your particular attention. Colonel Shirley is the next commander after you, wherefore if you should send such an officer he must conduct himself so as to appear only in quality of a friend or counsellor in the presence of Colonel Shirley: and his Royal Highness is of opinion that the officer must not produce or make mention of the commission you give him to command except in a case of absolute necessity.

" The ordering of these matters may be depended on, if the expedition at Crown Point can take place at the same time that Niagara is besieged.

"If after the Ohio expedition is ended it should be necessary for you to go with your whole force to Niagara it is the opinion of his Royal Highness that you should carefully endeavour to find a shorter way from the Ohio thither than that of the Lake; which however you are not to attempt under any pretense whatever without a moral certainty of being supplied with provisions, &c. As to your design of making yourself master of Niagara, which is of the greatest consequence, his Royal Highness recommends to you to leave nothing to chance in the prosecution of that enterpize.

"With regard to the reducing of Crown Point, the provincial troops being best acquainted with the country, will be of the most service.

"After the taking of this fort his Royal Highness advises you to consult with the Governors of the neighboring provinces, where it will be most proper to build a fort to cover the frontiers of those provinces.

"As to the forts which you think ought to be built (and of which they are perhaps too fond in that country), his Royal Highness recommends the building of them in such a manner, that they may not require a strong garrison. He is of opinion that you ought not to build considerable forts, cased with stone, till the plans and estimates thereof have been sent to England and approved of by the Government here. His Royal Highness thinks that stockaded forts, with pallisadoes and a good ditch, capable of containig 200 men or 400 upon an emergency, will be sufficient for the present.

"As Lieutenant Colonel Lawrence, who commands at Nova Scotia, hath long protracted the taking of Beau-Sejour, his Royal Highness advises you to consult with him, both with regard to the time and the manner of executing that design. In this enterprise his Royal Highness foresees that his majesty's ships may be of great service, as well by transporting the troops and warlike implements, as intercepting the stores and succors that might be sent to the French either by the Baye Françoise, or from Cape Breton by the Baye Verte on the other side of the Isthmus.

"With regard to your winter quarters after the operations of the campaign are finished, his Royal Highness recommends it

to you to examine whether the French will
not endeavor to make some attempts next
season and in what parts they will most
probably make them.   In this case it will
be most proper to canton your troops on
that side, at such distances, that they may
easily be assembled for the common
defence.   But you will be determined in
this matter by appearances, and the intelligence, which it hath been recommended
to you to procure by every method immediately after your landing.   It is unnecessary to put you in mind how careful you
must be to prevent being surprised.   His
Royal Highness imagines that your greatest
difficulty will be the subsisting of your
troops.   He therefore recommends it to
you to give your chief attention to this
matter, and to take proper measures relative
thereto with the Governors and with your
quartermasters and commissaries.

"I hope that the extraordinary supply
put on board the fleet, and the 1000 barrels
of beef destined for your use, will facilitate
and secure the supplying of your troops
with provisions.

"I think I have omitted nothing of all

the points wherein you desired to be informed: if there should be any intricate point unthought of, I desire you would represent it to me now, or at any other time; and I shall readily take it upon me to acquaint his Royal Highness thereof, and shall let you know his opinion on the subject.

" I wish you much success with all my heart; and as this success will infinitely rejoice all your friends, I desire you would be fully persuaded that no body will take greater pleasure in acquainting them thereof, than him, who is, &c."

If excuse is needed for offering in such detail these orders, it is that few men have ever suffered more heavily in reputation and in person because of the failures, misconceptions, and shortcomings of others than the man who received these orders and attempted to act upon them.

These instructions and the letter from the Duke of Cumberland make two things very clear: it is clear from the King's instructions (item 12) that the campaign to the Ohio Valley from Virginia was to be the important *coup* of the summer; the documents mentioned were to acquaint Braddock "with what has hitherto happened of a hostile Nature upon the Banks of that River." This is made more certain by one of the first sentences in the Duke of Cumberland's letter, "that immediately after your landing, you consider what artillery and other implements of war it will be necessary to transport to Will's Creek for your first operation on the Ohio." It is also clear that Braddock was helplessly dependent upon the success with which the American governors carried out the royal orders previously sent to them. They had been ordered to raise money and troops, provide provisions, open the necessary roads, supply carriages and horses, and conciliate and arm the Indian nations on the frontier. How far they were successful it will be proper to study later; for the moment, let us consider the destination of the little army that set sail, after innumerable delays, from the Downs December 21, 1754, led by the famed "Centurian" whose figure-head adorns Greenwich Hospital today.

Sending Braddock and his army to Virginia against the French on the Ohio was a natural blunder of immeasurable proportions. It was natural, because all eyes had been turned to Virginia by the activity of the Ohio Company, Washington's campaign of the preceding year, and the erection of Fort Cumberland on the farthest frontier. These operations gave a seeming importance to the Virginia route westward which was all out of harmony with its length and the facilities offered. "Before we parted," a friend of Braddock wrote concerning the General's last night in London, "the General told me that he should never see me more; for he was going with a handful of men to conquer whole nations; and to do this they must cut their way through unknown woods. He produced a map of the country, saying, at the same time, 'Dear Pop, we are sent like sacrifices to the altar.'" This gloomy prophecy was fulfilled with a fatal accuracy for which the choice of the Virginia route was largely responsible. Braddock's campaign had been fully considered in all its bearings in the royal councils, and the campaign through Virginia to Fort Duquesne seems to have been definitely decided upon. Even before Braddock had crossed half of the Atlantic his Quartermaster-General, St. Clair, had passed all the way through Virginia and Maryland to Fort Cumberland in carrying out orders issued to him before Braddock had reached England from Gibraltar. "Having procured from the Governors of Pennsylvania and Virginia and from other sources," writes Mr. Sargent, "all the maps and information that were obtainable respecting the country through which the expedition was to pass, he [St. Clair] proceeded in company with Governor Sharpe of Maryland upon a tour of inspection to Will's Creek." He inspected the Great Falls of the Potomac and laid plans for their being made passable for boats in which the army stores were to be shipped to Fort Cumberland, and had made contracts for the construction of the boats. He laid out a camp at Watkin's Ferry. It is doubtful whether Braddock had ever had one word to say in connection with all these plans which irrevocably doomed him to the almost impossible feat of making Fort

Cumberland a successful base of supplies and center of operations against the French. Moreover the Virginia route, being not only one of the longest on which Braddock could have approached the French, was the least supplied with any manner of wagons. "For such is the attention," wrote Entick, "of the Virginians towards their staple trade of tobacco, that they scarce raise as much corn, as is necessary for their own subsistence; and their country being well provided with water-carriage in great rivers an army which requires a large supply of wheel-carriages and beasts of burden, could not expect to be furnished with them in a place where they are not in general use."[5] "Their Produce is Tobacco," wrote one of Braddock's army, of the Virginians, "they are so attached to that, and their Avarice to raise it, makes them neglect every Comfort of Life." As has often been said, Carlisle in Pennsylvania would have made a far better center of operations than Fort Cumberland, and eventually it proved to be Pennsylvania wagons in which the stores

[5] Entick *History of the Late War*, vol. i., p. 142.

of the army were transported — without
which the army could not have moved
westward from Fort Cumberland one single
mile. " Mr. Braddock had neither provisions nor carriage for a march of so considerable a length, which was greatly increased
and embarrassed by his orders to take the
rout of Will's Creek; which road, as it
was the worst provided with provisions,
more troublesome and hazardous, and much
more about, than by way of Pennsylvania.'' [6]

Not to use superlatives, it would seem
that the American colonial governors and
St. Clair might have presented to Braddock
the difficulties of the Virginia route as compared with the Pennsylvania route early
enough to have induced the latter to make
Carlisle his base for the Ohio campaign;
but there is no telling now where the blunder was first made; a writer in *Gentleman's
Magazine* affirmed that the expedition was
" sent to *Virginia* instead of *Pennsylvania*,
to their insuperable disadvantage, merely
to answer the lucrative views of a friend
of the ministry, to whose share the remit-

[6] *History of the Late War*, vol. i., p. 142.

tances would then fall at the rate of 2½ *per cent* profit.'' [7]

Even the suspicion of such treachery as sending Braddock to Virginia to indulge the purse of a favorite is the more revolting because of the suggestion in the letter from the Duke of Cumberland that Braddock, personally, favored an attack on Fort Niagara — which, it has been universally agreed, was the thing he should have done. '' As to *your design* of making yourself master of Niagara '' — the italics are mine — wrote Cumberland; and, though he refers at the beginning to their numerous interviews, this is the sole mention throughout the letter of any opinion or plan of Braddock's. '' Had General *Braddock* made it his first business to secure the command of lake Ontario, which he might easily have done soon enough to have stopt the *force* that was sent from *Canada* to *Du Quesne*, that fort must have been surrendered to him upon demand; and had he gone this way to it, greater part of that vast sum

[7] *Gentleman's Magazine*, vol. 75, p. 389 (1755); also *A Review of the Military Operations in North America*, London, 1757, p. 35.

might have been saved to the nation, which was expended in making a waggon road, through the woods and mountains, the way he went."[8] Yet Cumberland's orders were distinct to go to Niagara by way of Virginia and Fort Duquesne.

Horace Walpole's characterization of Braddock is particularly graphic and undoubtedly just — "desperate in his fortune, brutal in his behavior, obstinate in his sentiments, intrepid and capable."[9] The troops given him for the American expedition were well suited to bring out every defect in his character; these were the fragments of the 44th and 48th regiments, then stationed in Ireland. Being deficient (even in time of peace), both had to be recruited up to five hundred men each. The campaign was unpopular and the recruits secured were of the worst type — "who, had they not been in the army, would probably have been in Bridewell [prison]." Walpole wrote, "the troops allotted to him most ill-chosen, being draughts of the most worthless in some Irish regiments, and

---

[8] *A letter relating to the Ohio Defeat*, p. 14.

[9] Walpole's *Memoirs of George II*, vol. ii., p. 29.

anew disgusted by this species of banish-
ment." [10]   " The mutinous Spirit of the
Men encreases," wrote an officer of Braddock's army during the march to Fort
Duquesne, " but we will get the better of
that, we will see which will be tired first,
they of deserving Punishments, or we of
inflicting them . . they are mutinous,
and this came from a higher Spring than
the Hardships here, for they were tainted
in *Ireland* by the factious Cry against
the L— L— Ld G—, and the Primate;
the wicked Spirit instilled there by Pamphlets and Conversation, got amongst the
common Soldiers, who, tho' they are *Englishmen*, yet are not the less stubborn and
mutinous for that."

Thus the half-mutinous army, and its
" brutal," " obstinate," " intrepid," and
" capable " commander fared on across the
sea to Virginia during the first three months
of the memorable year of 1755.   By the
middle of March the entire fleet had
weighed anchor in the port of Alexandria,
Virginia.

[10] Walpole's *Memoirs of George II*, vol. ii., p. 29;
also London *Evening Post*, September 9–11, 1755.

The situation could not be described better than Entick has done in the following words: " Put all these together, what was extraordinary in his [Braddock's] conduct, and what was extraordinary in the way of the Service, there could be formed no good idea of the issue of such an untoward expedition.''

CHAPTER III

WHAT it was that proved to be " extraordinary in the way of the Service" General Braddock soon discovered, and it is a fair question whether, despite all that has been written concerning his unfitness for his position, another man with one iota less "spirit" than Braddock could have done half that Braddock did.

The Colonies were still quite asleep to their danger; the year before, Governor Dinwiddie had been at his wits' end to raise in Virginia a few score men for Fry and Washington, and had at last succeeded by dint of drafts and offers of bounty in western lands. Pennsylvania was hopelessly embroiled in the then unconstitutional question of equal taxation of proprietary estates. The New York assembly was, and not without reason, clannish in giving men and money for use only within her own borders. It is interesting to notice the early flashes of lurking revolutionary fire in the Colonies when the mother-country attempted to wield them to serve her own politic schemes. Braddock was perhaps one of the first Englishmen to suggest the taxation of America and, within a year, Walpole wrote concerning instructions sent to a New York Governor, that they "seemed better calculated for the latitude of Mexico and for a Spanish tribunal than for a free rich British Settlement," and in such opulence and of such haughtiness, that suspicion had long been conceived of their meditating to throw off their dependence on their mother country."[11] It would have been well for the provinces if they had postponed for a moment their struggle against English methods, and planned as earnestly for the success of English arms as they did when defeat opened the floodgates of murder and pillage all along their wide frontiers. But it is not possible to more than mention here the struggles

[11] Walpole's *Memoirs of George II*, vol. i., p. 397; Sargent's *History of Braddock's Expedition*, p. 153, note.

between the short-sighted assemblies and the short-sighted royal governors. The practical result, so far as Braddock was concerned, was the ignoring, for the greater part, of all the instructions sent from London. This meant that Braddock was abandoned to the fate of carrying out orders wretchedly planned under the most trying circumstances conceivable. Instead of having everything prepared for him, he found almost nothing prepared, and on what had been done he found he could place no dependence. Little wonder the doomed man has been remembered as a " brute " in America! To have shouldered the blame for the lethargy of the Colonies, for the jealousy of their governors, and for the wretchedness of the orders given Braddock, would have made any man brutish in word and action. Pennsylvanians have often accused Washington of speaking like a " brute " when, no doubt in anger, he exclaimed that the officials of that Province should have been flogged for their indifference; they were, God knows,— but by the Indians after Braddock's defeat.

The desperateness of Braddock's situa-

tion became very plain by the middle of
April, when the Governors of the Colonies
met at his request at the camp at Alexandria to determine upon the season's campaigns. But it was not until later that he
knew the full depths of his unfortunate
situation. As early as March 18 Braddock wrote Sir Thomas Robinson a most
discouraging letter, but on April 19,
after the Governors' Council, another
letter to Robinson shows the exact situation. As to the fund which the Colonies
had been ordered to raise, the Governors
" gave it as their unanimous opinion that
such a Fund can never be establish'd in the
Colonies without the Aid of Parliament." [12]
They were therefore " unanimously of the
Opinion that the Kings Service in the
Colonies, and the carrying on of the present
Expedition must be at a stand, unless the
General shall think proper to make use of
his Credit upon the Government at home to
defray the Expense of all the Operations
under his Direction." [12] In Braddock's

[12] Minutes taken " At a Council at the Camp at Alexandria in Virginia, April 14, 1755." Public Records
Office, London: *America and West Indies*, No. 82.

letter of April 19 he affirms " The £20,000 voted in Virginia has been expended tho not yet collected; Pennsylvania and Maryland still refuse to contribute anything; New York has raised £5,000 Currency for the use of the Troops whilst in that province, which I have directed to be applied for the particular Service of the Garrison at Oswego. . . I shall march from this place for Frederick tomorrow Morning in my Way to Will's Creek, where I should have been before this time, had I not been prevented by waiting for the artillery, from which I still fear further delays. I hope to be upon the mountains early in May and some time in June to have it in my power to dispatch an Express with some Account of the Event of our operations upon the Ohio." [13] The disappointed man was not very sanguine of success, but adds, " I hope, Sir, there is good prospect of success in every part of the plan I have laid before you, but it is certain every single attempt is more likely to succeed from the Extensiveness of it." [13] By this he meant that

[13] Braddock's MS. Letters, Public Records Office, London: *America and West Indies*, No. 82.

the French, attacked at several points at once, would not be able to send reinforcements from one point to another.

But more serious disappointments awaited Braddock — a great part of the definite promises made by Governor Dinwiddie were never to be realized. The governor and Sir John St. Clair had promised Braddock that twenty-five hundred horses and two hundred wagons would be in readiness at Fort Cumberland to transport the army stores across the mountains, and that a large quantity of beeves and other provisions would be awaiting the army through July and August. Braddock was also promised the support of a large force of Indians and, conformably to his orders, had been careful to send the usual presents to the tribes in question. He soon learned, however, that the short-sighted Assemblies of both Virginia and Pennsylvania had already alienated the Indians whom they should have attached to their cause, and but a handful were faithful now when the crisis had come; for the faithfulness of these few Braddock was perhaps largely in debt to Washington, whom they followed during the campaign of the preceding year. As to the details of his miserable situation, nothing is of more interest than the frank letter written by Braddock to Sir John Robinson from Fort Cumberland, June 5:

" I had the Honor of writing to you from Frederick the latter end of April.

" On the 10th of May I arriv'd at this place, and on the 17th the train join'd me from Alexandria after a March of twenty seven days, having met with many more Delays and Difficulties than I had even apprehended, from the Badness of the Roads, Scarcity of Forage, and a general Want of Spirit in the people to forward the Expedition.

" I have at last collected the whole Force with which I propose to march to the Attack of Fort Duquesne, amounting to about two thousand effective Men, eleven hundred of which Number are Americans of the southern provinces, whose slothful and languid Disposition renders them very unfit for Military Service. I have employ'd the properest officers to form and discipline them and great pains has and shall be taken to make them as useful as possible.

"When I first came to this place I design'd to have refresh'd the Troops by a few days Rest, but the Disappointments I have met with in procuring the Number of Wagons and Horses necessary for my March over the Mountains have detained me near a Month.

"Before I left Williamsburg I was informed by the Deputy Quarter Master general, who was then at this Fort, that 2500 Horses and 200 Wagons might be depended upon from Virginia and Maryland, but as I had the utmost reason to fear a Disappointment from my daily Experience of the Falsehood of every person with whom I was concern'd, I therefore before I left Frederick, desired Mr. Franklin, postmaster of Pennsylvania, and a Man of great Influence in that Province, to contract for 150 Waggons and a Number of Horses, which he has executed with great punctuality and Integrity, and is almost the only Instance of Ability and Honesty I have known in these provinces; His Waggons and Horses have all joined me, and are indeed my whole Dependence, the great promises of Virginia and Maryland having

produc'd only about twenty Waggons and two hundred Horses: With the Number I now have I shall be enabled with the utmost difficulty to move from this place, marching with one half of the provision I entended and having been oblig'd to advance a large Detachment in order to make a Deposite of provisions upon the Alliganey Mountains about five days March from me.

"It would be endless, Sir, to particularize the numberless Instances of the Want of public and private Faith, and of the most absolute Disregard of all Truth, which I have met with in carrying on of His Majesty's Service on this continent. I cannot avoid adding one or two Instances to what I have already given.

"A Contract made by the Governor of Virginia for 1100 Beeves was laid before me to be delivered in July and August for the subsistence of the Troops, which Contract he had entered into upon the Credit of twenty thousand pounds Currency voted by the Assembly for the Service of the Expedition. Depending upon this I regulated my Convoys accordingly, and a few days since the Contractors inform'd me that the Assembly had refus'd to fulfill the Governors Engagements, and the Contract was consequently void: as it was an Affair of the greatest Importance, I immediately offer'd to advance the Money requir'd by the Terms of the Contract, but this the Contractor rejected, unless I would pay him one third more; and postpone the Delivery of the Beeves two Months, at which time they would have been of no use to me.

"Another Instance is the Agent employ'd in the Province of Maryland for furnishing their Troops with provision, who delivered it in such Condition that it is all condemn'd upon a Survey, and I have been obliged to replace it by sending to the Distance of an hundred Miles.

"This Behavior in the people does not only produce infinite Difficulty in carrying on His Majesty's Service but also greatly increases the Expense of it, the Charge thereby occasion'd in the Transportation of provision and Stores through an unsettled Country (with which even the Inhabitants of the lower parts are entirely unac-

quainted) and over a continued succession
of Mountains, is many times more than
double the original Cost of them; for this
reason I am obliged to leave a Quantity of
provision at Alexandria, which would be of
great Service to use at this place. The
Behaviour of the Governments appears to
me to be without excuse, but it may be
some Extenuation of the Guilt of the lower
Class of people, that upon former occasions
their assistance in publick has been ill
rewarded, and their payments neglected;
the bad Effects of which proceeding we
daily experience.

"As I have His Majesty's Orders to
establish as much as possible a good understanding with the Indians, I have gathered
some from the Frontier of Pennsylvania
chiefly of the Six Nations, with whom I
have had two or three Conferences, and
have given them proper Presents; the
Number already with me is about fifty, and
I have some hopes of more: Upon my first
Arrivall in America, I received strong
assurances of the assistance of a great
Number of Southern Indians, which I have
entirely lost through the Misconduct of the

Government of Virginia: And indeed the whole Indian Affairs have been so imprudently and dishonestly conducted, that it was with the greatest difficulty I could gain a proper Confidence with those I have engag'd, and even that could not be attain'd, nor can be preserv'd without a great Expense.

"The Nature of the Country prevents all Communication with the French but by Indians, and their Intelligence is not much to be depended upon; they all agree the Number of French now in Fort Duquesne is very inconsiderable, but that they pretend to expect large Reinforcements.

"I have an Account of the arrival of the two thousand Arms for the New England Forces, and that they are sailed for Nova Scotia. Batteaus and Boats are preparing for the Forces destined to the Attacks of Niagara and Crown Point, but the province of New York, which by its situation must furnish the greater part, do not act with so much vigor as I could wish.

"In order to secure a short and easy Communication with the province of Pensilvania, after the Forces have pass'd the

Alligany Mountains, I have apply'd to
Governor Morris to get a Road cut from
Shippensburg in that Province to the River
Youghyaughani; up which he informs me he
has set a proper Number of Men at work,
and that it will be compleated in a Month:
This I look upon to be an Affair of the
greatest Importance, as well for securing
future Supplies of Provisions, as for obtain-
ing more speedy Intelligence of what passes
in the Northern Colonies.[14]

" I wait now for the last Convoy and
shall, if I do not meet with further Disappointments, begin my March over the
Alleghaney Mountains in about five days.
The Difficulties we have to meet with by
the best Accounts are very great; the
Distance from hence to the Forts is an
hundred and ten miles, a Road to be cut
and made the whole way with infinite Toil
and Labor, over rocky Mountains of an
excessive Height and Steepness, and many
Stoney Creeks and Rivers to cross."

Braddock's army under Halket and Dun-

[14] For these early routes through Pennsylvania, par-
tially opened in 1755, see *Historic Highways of America*, vol. v., chap. i.

bar proceeded to Fort Cumberland from Alexandria by various routes. Governor Sharpe had had a new road built from Rock Creek to Fort Cumberland;[15] this was probably Dunbar's route and is given as follows in Braddock's Orderly Books:[16]

MILES

To Rock Creek [17] .	—
To Owen's Ordinary .	15
To Dowdens .	15
To Frederick	15
From Fred^k on ye road to Conogogee.	17
From that halting place to Conogogee .	18
From Conogogee to John Evens	16
To the Widow Baringer .	18
To George Polls .	9
To Henry Enock's	15
To Cox's at ye mouth of little Cacaph	12
To Col. Cresaps .	8
To Wills Creek .	16
	174

[15] *Maryland Archives;* Correspondence of Governor Sharpe, vol. i., pp. 77 and 97.

[16] Preserved at the Congressional Library, Washington.

[17] Eight miles from Alexandria. See Note 26.

Halket's regiment went from Alexandria
to Winchester, Virginia by the following
route as given in Braddock's Orderly Books:

	MILES
To yᵉ old Court House . . .	18
To Mʳ Colemans on Sugar Land Run where there is Indian Corn &c.	12
To Mʳ Miners	15
To Mʳ Thompson yᵉ Quaker wh is 3000 wt corn . . .	12
To Mʳ They's yᵉ Ferry of Shanh	17
From Mʳ They's to Winchester	23
	97

At Winchester Halket was only five miles
distant from "Widow Baringer's" on
Dunbar's road from Frederick to Fort Cumberland.

One of the few monuments of Braddock's
days stands beside the Potomac, within the
limits of the city of Washington. It is a
gigantic rock, the "Key of Keys," now
almost lost to sight and forgotten. It may
still be found, and efforts are on foot to
have it appropriately marked. It is known
in tradition as "Braddock's Rock" — on
the supposition that here some of Brad-

dock's men landed just below the mouth
of Rock Creek en route to Frederick and
Fort Cumberland. It is unimportant
whether the legend is literally true.[18] A
writer, disputing the legend, yet affirms
that the public has reason " to require that
the destructive hand of man be stayed, and
that the remnants of the ancient and historic rock should be rescued from oblivion."
The rock may well bear the name of Braddock, as the legend has it. Nothing could
be more typical of the man — grim, firm,
unreasoning, unyielding.

[18] Arguments pro and con have been interestingly
summed up by Dr. Marcus Benjamin of the U. S. National Museum, in a paper read before the Society of
Colonial Dames in the District of Columbia April 12,
1899, and by Hugh T. Taggart in the *Washington Star*,
May 16, 1896. For a description of routes converging
on Braddock's Road at Fort Cumberland see Gen. Wm.
P. Craighill's article in the *West Virginia Historical
Magazine*, vol. ii, no. 3 (July, 1902), p. 31. Cf. pp.
179–181.

CHAPTER IV

A SEAMAN'S JOURNAL

ONE of the most interesting documents relative to Braddock's expedition is a *Journal* kept by one of the thirty seamen sent with Braddock by Commodore Keppel. The original manuscript was presented by Colonel Macbean to the Royal Artillery Library, Woolwich, and is first published here.

An expanded version of this document was published in Winthrop Sargent's *History of Braddock's Expedition*, entitled " The Morris Journal " — so called because it was in the possession of the Rev. Francis-Orpen Morris, Nunburnholme Rectory, Yorkshire, who had published it in pamphlet form.[19] Concerning its authorship Mr.

[19] London, Groombridge & Sons, 1854. Mr. Morris, in footnotes, gave what he considered any important variations of the original manuscript from the expanded version he was editing; Mr. Sargent reproduced these notes, without having seen the original.

Sargent says, " I do not know who was the author of this Journal: possibly he may have been of the family of Capt. Hewitt. He was clearly one of the naval officers detached for this service by Com. Keppel, whom sickness detained at Fort Cumberland during the expedition."[20]

A comparison of the expanded version with the original here printed shows that the " Morris Journal" was written by Engineer Harry Gordon of the 48th Artillery. The entry in the expanded version for June 2 reads: " Col. Burton, Capt. Orme, Mr Spendlowe and self went out to reconnoitre the road." [21] In the original, under the same date, we read: " Colonel Burton, Capt. Orme, Mr Engineer Gordon & Lieut Spendelow were order'd to reconnoitre the Roads." Why Mr. Gordon desired to suppress his name is as inexplicable as the failure of the Rev. Francis-Orpen Morris, who compared the expanded and the original manuscripts, to announce it. The proof is made more sure by the fact that Mr. Gordon usually refers to himself as an " Engineer,"

[20] *History of Braddock's Expedition*, p. 359, note.
[21] *Id.*

as in the entry for June 3: " This morning an Engineer and 100 men began working on the new road. . . ." In the
original the name is given: " Engineer
Gordon with 100 Pioneers began to break
Ground on the new Road. . . ." [22] He
refers to himself again on July 9 as " One
of our Engineers ": " One of our Engineers,
who was in the front of the Carpenters
marking the road, saw the Enemy first." [23]
It is well known that Gordon first caught
sight of the enemy and the original journal
affirms this to have been the case: " Mr
Engineer Gordon was the first Man that
saw the Enemy." Mr. Sargent said the
author " was clearly one of the naval officers detached . . . by Com. Keppel."
Though Mr. Gordon, as author, imperson-
ated a seaman, there is certainly very much
more light thrown on the daily duties of an
engineer than on those of a sailor; there is
far more matter treating of cutting and
marking Braddock's Road than of handling

[22] Mr. Gordon evidently used the word " self " in his
entry of June 3 to throw any too curious reader off the
track.

[23] *History of Braddock's Expedition*, p. 387.

ropes and pulleys. It is also significant
that Gordon, from first to last, was near
the seamen and had all the necessary information for composing a journal of which one
of them might have been the author. He
was in Dunbar's regiment on the march from
Alexandria — as were the seamen. He,
with the carpenters, was possibly brigaded
in the Second Brigade, with the seamen,
and in any case he was with the van of the
army on the fatal ninth as were the seamen.

As to the authorship of the original journal the document gives no hint. From Mr.
Gordon's attempt to cover his own identity
by introducing the word " self " in the
latter part of the entry of June 3, it might
be supposed the original manuscript was
written by the " Midshipman " referred to
under that date in the original journal.
But the two midshipmen given as naval
officers in the expedition, Haynes and Tal-
bot, were killed in the defeat.[24]

The original journal which follows is of
interest because of the description of the
march of Dunbar's brigade through Maryland and Virginia to Fort Cumberland.

[24] *History of Braddock's Expedition*, p. 365.

The remainder was evidently composed from descriptions given by officers after their return to Fort Cumberland: [25]

Extracts from

A Journal of the Proceedings of the Detachment of Seamen, ordered by Commodore Kepple, to Afsist on the late Expedition to the *Ohio* with an impartial Account of the late Action on the Banks of the *Monongohela*

[25] In the Gordon Journal, under the date of June 10, there are two entries. One seems to have been Gordon's and reads: " The Director of the Hospital came to see me in Camp, and found me so ill . . . I went into the Hospital, & the Army marched with the Train &c., and as I was in hopes of being able to follow them in a few days, I sent all my baggage with the Army." Without doubt this was Gordon's entry, as no sailor could have had sufficient baggage to warrant such a reference as this, while an engineer's " kit " was an important item. Then follow two entries (June 24 and 26) evidently recorded by one who remained at Fort Cumberland, and a second entry under the date of June 10, which is practically the first sentence of the entry under the same date in the original manuscript, and which has the appearance of being the genuine record made by the sailor detained at Fort Cumberland. The confusion of these entries in the Gordon Journal makes it very evident that one author did not compose them. The two entries for June 10 are typical of " Mr Engineer Gordon " and an unknown sailor.

the 9th of July 1755. as related by some of the Principal Officers that day in the Field, from the 10th April 1755 to the 18th Aug[st]. when the Detachment of Seamen embark'd on board His Majisty's Ship Guarland at Hampton in Virginia

April 10th Orders were given to March to Morrow with 6 Companies of S[r] P. Halket's Regiment for *Winchester* towards *Will's Creeks;* April 11th Yesterdays Orders were Countermanded and others given to furnish Eight days Provisions, to proceed to *Rock's Creek*[26] (8 Miles from Alexandria) in the Sea Horse & Nightingale Boats; April 12th: Arrived at *Rock's Creek* 5 Miles from the lower falls of *Potomack* & 4 Miles from the Eastern branch of it; where we encamped with Colonel Dunbars Regiment

April 13th: Employed in loading Waggon's with Stores Provisions and all other conviniences very dear *Rock's Creek* a very pleasant Situation.

[26] This form of the name of the modern Rock Creek is significant and is not given in the expanded form of this journal. "Rock's Creek" suggests that the great bowlder known as "Braddock's Rock" was a landmark in 1755 and had given the name to the stream which entered the Potomac near it.

April 14th: Detachment of Seamen were order'd to March in the Front: arrived at M^r. Lawrence Owen's: 15 Miles from *Rock's Creek;* and encamp'd upon good Ground 8 Miles from the Upper falls of *Potomack*

April 15th: Encamp'd on the side of a Hill near M^r. Michael Dowden's;[27] 15 Miles from M^r. Owen's, in very bad Ground and in 1½ foot Snow

April 16th: Halted, but found it extreamly difficult to get either Provisions or Forrage.

April 17th: March'd to *Fredericks Town;* 15 Miles from Dowden's, the road very Mountanious, March'd 11 Miles, when we came to a River call'd *Monskiso*, which empties itself into the *Potomack*; it runs very rapid; and is, after hard Rain, 13 feet deep: We ferried over in a Float for that purpose. This Town has not been settled Above 7. Years; there are 200 Houses & 2 Churches 1 Dutch, 1 English;[28] the inhab-

[27] The use of full names in this journal is strong evidence that it is the original.

[28] The Gordon Journal assiduously reverses every such particular as this; it reads here: "there are about 200 houses and 2 churches, one English, one Dutch."

itants chiefly Dutch, Industrious, but imposing People; Provisions & Forrage in Plenty.

April 18th: Encamp'd with a New York Company under the Command of Captain Gates, at the North End of the Town, upon very good Ground

April 19th: Exercising Recuits, & airing the Tents: several Waggons arrived with Ordnance Stores, heavy Dews at Night occasion it to be very unwholsome

April 20th: Nothing Material happen'd

April 21st: The General attended by Captains Orme, Morris and Secretary Shirley; with S[r] John S[t] Clair; arrived at Head Quarters.

April 24th inactive [29].

April 25th: Ordnance Stores Arrived, with 80 Recruits for the 2 Regiments

April 27th: Employ'd in preparing Harnefs for the Horses

[29] Though in almost every instance the Gordon Journal gives a more wordy account of each day's happenings, it *never gives a record for a day that is omitted by this journal*, as April 22, 23, and 28; at times, however, a day is omitted in that journal that is accounted for in this; see entries for May 9 and May 25 — neither of which did Mr. Morris give in his footnotes, though the latter was of utmost significance.

April 29th: March'd to M[r]. Walker's 18 Miles from *Fredericks Town*; paſs'd the South Ridge, commonly called the Blue Ridge or *Shanandoh Mountains* Very easy Ascent and a fine Prospect . . no kind of Refreshment

April 30th: March'd to *Connecochiag*; 16 Miles from M[r] Walker's, Close by the *Potomack*, a very fine Situation, where we found all the Artillery Stores preparing to go by Water to Wills Creek

May 1st: Employed in ferrying (over the *Potomack*) the Army Baggage into Virginia in 2 Floats and 5 Batteaux; The Army March'd to M[r] John Evans, 16 Miles from y[e] *Potomack* and 20 Miles from Winchester, where we Encamp'd, and had tolerable good living with Forrage; the roads begin to be very indifferent

May 2nd: Halted and sent the Horses to Grafs

May 3[d]: March'd to Widdow Barringers 18 Miles from M[r]. Evans; the day was so exciſsive hot, that many Officers and Men could not Arrive at their Ground until Evening, this is 5 Miles from Winchester and a fine Situation

May 4th: March'd to M[r]. Pots 9 Miles from the Widdow's where we were refresh[t] with Vinison and wild Turkeys the Roads excefsive bad.

May 5th: March'd to M[r]. Henry Enocks, a place called the *forks of Cape Capon*, 16 Miles from M[r]. Pots; over prodigious Mountains, and between the Same we crofs'd a Run of Water in 3 Miles distance, 20 times after marching 15 Miles we came to a River called *Kahepatin* where the Army ferried over, We found a Company of S[r] Peter Halkets Regiment waiting to escort the Train of Artillery to *Wills Creek*

May 6th: Halted, as was the Custom to do every third day, The Officers for pafsing away the time, made Horse Races and agreed that no Horse should Run over 11 Hands and to carry 14 Stone

May 7th: March'd to M[r]. Coxs's by the side of y[e] *Potomack* 12 Miles from M[r]. Enock's, and Encamped we crofs'd another run of Water 19 Times in 2 Miles Roads bad.

May 8th: Ferried over the River into *Maryland*; and March'd to M[r]. Jacksons, 8 Miles from M[r]. Coxs's where we found a

Maryland Company encamp'd in a fine
Situation on the Banks of the *Potomack*;
with clear'd ground about it; there lives
Colonel Creſsop, a Rattle Snake, Colonel,
and a D—d Rascal; calls himself a Fron-
tierman, being nearest the *Ohio*; he had a
Summons some time since from the French
to retire from his Settlement, which they
claim'd as their property, but he refused it
like a man of Spirit; [30] This place is the
Track of Indian Warriours, when going to
War, either to the N°ward, or S°ward He
hath built a little Fort round his House,
and is resolved to keep his Ground. We
got plenty of Provisions &cᵃ. The General
arrived with Captains Orme and Morris,
with Secretary Shirley and a Company of
light Horse for his Guard, under the Command of Capᵗ. Stewart, the General lay at
the Colonels.

[30] The words " from the French " are omitted in the
Gordon Journal, which makes the entry utterly devoid
of any meaning — unless that Cresap had been ordered
to retire by the Ohio Company! Cresap in that document is called " a vile Rascal "; cf. Pennsylvania *Colonial Records*, vol. vi., p. 400. For eulogy of Cresap
see *Ohio State Archæological and Historical Publications*, vol. xi.

May 9th: Halted and made another Race to amuse the General

Do. 10th: March'd to *Will's Creek*; and Encamp'd on a Hill to the Etward of the Fort, when the General past the Troops; Colonel Dunbar informed them, that there were a number of Indians at *Wills Creek*, that were Friends to the English therefore it was the Generals positive Orders, that they should not be Molested upon any account, upon the Generals Arrival at the Fort, He was Saluted with 17. Guns, and we found 100 Indian Men, Women & Children with 6 Companies of Sr Peter Halkets Regiment, 9 Virginian Companies and a Maryland Company.

May 11th: *Fort Cumberland*, is Situated within 200 Yards of *Wills Creek* on a Hill 400 Yards from the *Potomack*, it's greatest length from East to West is 200 Yards, and breadth 40 it is built with Loggs drove into the Ground: and 12 feet above it Embrazures are cut for 12 Guns which are 4. Pounders, though 10 are only Mounted with loopholes for small Arms; The Indians were greatly surprised at the regular way of our Soldiers Marching and our Numbers.

I would willingly say something of the customs & manners of them, but they are hardly to be described.   The Men are tall, well made and Active, but not strong; The Women not so tall yet well proportion'd & have many Children; they paint themselves in different Manners; Red, Yellow & Black intermixt, the Men have the outer Rim of their Ears cut; and hanging by a little bit at Top and bottom: they have also a Tuft of Hair left at Top of their Heads, drefs'd with Feathers. . .   Their Match Coat which is their chief Cloathing, is a thick Blanket thrown round them; and instead of Shoes wear Mekosins, which laces round the foot and Ankle . . .   their manner of carrying Children are by lacing them on a Board, and tying them with a broad Bandage with a place to rest their feet, and Boards over their Heads to keep the Sun off and this is Slung to the Womens backs. These people have no Idea of a Superior Being or of Religion and I take them to be the most ignorant, as to the Knowledge of the World and things, of any Creatures living.   When it becomes dark they Return to their Camp, which is [nigh] Woods, and

Dance for some Time with making the
most hidious Noise.

May 12th: Orders for a Council of War
at the Head Quarters when the Indians
came, and were received by the Guard with
Rested Arms, an Interpreter was directed
to tell them that their Brothers, the English, who were their friends were come to
afsist them, that every misunderstanding
in past times, should now be buried under
that great Mountain (which was close by)
and Accordingly the Ceremony was perform'd in giving them a string of Wampum
or Beads; and the following speech was
made, to Afsure them that this string or Belt
of Wampum was a suriety of our Friendship; and likewise a Declaration, that
every one, who were Enemies to them, were
consequently so to us. The Interpretor
likewise afsured them, the we had a Considerable Number of Men to the N°Ward,
under the Commands of our great War
Captains Generals, Shirley, Pepperel &
Johnson that were making preparations for
War to settle them happily in their Countries, and make the French both ashamed
& hungry, however, should any Indians

absent themselves they would be deem'd
our Enimies & treated as such; The Gen.
erals moreover told them, he should have
presents for them soon, and would then
make them another Speech, after which he
parted with giving a Dram round.

May 13th: The Indian Camp were ¼
Miles from the Fort which I went to visit
their Houses are composed of 2 Stakes,
drove into the Ground, with a Ridge Pole
& Bark of Trees laid down the sides of it,
w[ch]. is all they have to Shelter them from
the Weather.   .   .   The Americans &
Seamen Exercising.

May 14th: Inactive in our Camp. I went
to the Indian to see them Dance which they
do once or twice a Year round a Fire, first
the Women dance, whilst the Men are
Sitting, and then every Women takes out
her Man; dances with him; lays with him
for a Week, and then Returns to her proper
Husband, & lives with him.[31]

May 15th: 22 Casks of Beef were Surveyed
and condemn'd [32]

[31] This is given for the 13th in the Gordon Journal.
[32] The Gordon Journal: "Mr Spendlow and self surveyed 22 casks of beef, and condemned it, which we
reported to the General."

D°. 16th: Arrived Lt. Col°. Gage with 2
Companies, and the last Division of the
Train, consisting of 8 Field Pieces; 4
Howitzers and a Number of Cohorns, with
42 Store Waggons Capt. Bromley of Sr P.
Halkets Regimt. died May 17th: Orders for
the Funeral.

May 18th. Capt. Bromley was interred
with great Solemnity [38] —19th: the Indians
came to the Generals Tent when he made
them a speech to this Effect; that they
would send away immediately their Wives
& Children to Pensilvania, and take up the
Hatchet against the French, that the great
King of England their Father had sent
their Wives & Children such & such presents, and he had Ordered Arms, Ammunition &ca. to be delivered to their Warriors,
and exprefsd a Concern for their ½ King
killed last year — the presents consisted of
Shrouds; Rings, Beads, Linnen, Knives,
Wire & paint, they seem'd pleased, received
their presents with 3 Belts & String of

---

[38] Two chaplains accompanied the two Regiments
Philip Hughes was chaplain of the 44th and Lieut. John
Hamilton of the 48th. The latter was wounded in the
defeat.

Wampum, and promised an Answer the next day in the Evening they Danced and made a most terrible Noise to shew were mightily pleased.

May 20th: Capt. Gates March'd into Camp with his New York Compy. The Indians met at the Generals Tent, and told him they were highly Obliged to the Great King their Father, for sending such Numbers of Men to fight for them, and they moreover promise to Join them, and do what was in their power by reconnoitring the Country, & bringing Intelligence, they were likewise oblidged to the General for exprefsing his Concern for the lofs of their ½ King his Brother, and for the Presents he had made their Families. Their Chiefs Names were as follows

1st: Monicatoha their Mentor, 2d Belt of Wampum, or white Thunder, who always keep the Wampum, and has a Daughter call'd bright Lightning 3d: The great Tree and Silver Heels, Jimy Smith and Charles all. belonging to the 6 Nations, The General Afsured them of his Friendship and gave his Honour, that he never would deceive them, after which they sung

their Song of War, put themselves into odd
postures, wth Shouting and making an
uncommon Noise, declaring the French to
be their pepetual Enemies, which they
never had done before, then the General
took the Indians to the Park of Artillery,
Ordered 3 Howtz^rs. 3 : 12 pounders to be
Fired, the Drums beating & Fifes playing
the point of War, which astonish^t but
pleased the Indians greatly. they afterwards Retired to their own Camp to eat a
Bullock and Dance in their usual manner,
with shewing how they fight and Scalp,
and exprefsing in their Dance, the exploits
& Warlike Actions of their Ancestors and
themselves — Arrived 80 Waggons from
Pensylvania with Stores; and 11 likewise
from Philidelpha with Liquors, Tea,
Sugar, Coffe &c. to the Amount of 400£
With 20 Horses, as presents to the Officers
of the 2 Regiments — An Indian came in 6
days from the French Fort, and afsured us
they have only 50 Men in the Fort, however they expected 900 more soon, yet they
purpose blowing it up whenever the Army
Appears — as this Indian was one of the
Delawars, who never were our Friends he

was suspected to be a Rogue — 100 Carpenters were Employed in making a Float, building a Magazine & squaring Timber to make a Bridge over *Wills Creek*, The Smiths were making Miners Tools, The Bakers were baking Biscuit, and every thing was getting ready for a March.

May 21st: A Troop of light Horse & 2 Companies of Sr P. Halkets Regimt. under the Command of Major Chapman came in from Winchester

May 22d: The Indians had Arms & Cloaths delivered to them

Do. 23d: The 2 Regiments were Exercised & went through their Formings

Do. 24th: Employed in Transporting the large Timber to the Fort, The Army consists of 2 Regiments, Each 700 Men; 2 *New York*, 1 Independent *Carolina* Companies of 100 Men, 9 *Virginia* 1 *Maryland* Companies of 50 Men; 1 Compy. of Artillery of 60 & 30 Seamen

May 25th: Preparations for Marching: 2 Men of Sr P. Halkets were Drum'd out, and received 1000 lashes Each for Theft.

May 27th: The Companies employed in loading 100 Waggons wth. Provisions, A

Captains Guard March'd for *Winchester* to Escort Provisions to Camp — several *Delawar* Indians came into Camp.

May 28th: The *Delawar* Indians Afsembled at the Generals Tent and told him they were come to Afsist him, but desired to know his Intention the General thank'd them, and said that he should March in a few days for Fort Dec Quisne, The Indians then replyed, they would return home, Collect their Warriors and meet them on his March.

May 29th: Major Chapman with a Detachment of 600 Soldiers March'd with 2 Field Pieces and 50 Waggons full of Provisions when Sr John St Clair, 2 Engineers, Lieut. Spendelow & 6 Seamen with some Indians were Order'd to clean the Roads for them,

May 30th: March'd in, Capt. Dobbs with a *North Carolina* Company

June 1st: The Detachment got 15 Miles though the Roads were very bad; Lieut. Spendelow returned with his 6 Seamen.

June 2d: Colonel Burton, Capt. Orme, Mr. Engineer Gordon [34] & Lieut. Spendelow were order'd to reconnoitre the Roads, the

[34] The entry of Gordon Journal reads: " Col. Burton, Capt. Orme, Mr. Spendlowe and self . ."

latter reported that he had found a tolerable Road, which might avoid the bad Mountain that they would otherwise be obliged to pafs; and accordingly it was determined to March the Army that way, it being only 2 Miles about.

June 3ᵈ: Engineer Gordon [35] with 100 Pioneers began to break Ground on the new Road, when Lieuᵗ. Spendelow, 1 Midshipman [36] & 10 Men were sent to the Place that leads into the Old Road, cleard away and compleated 1 Mile,

June 4ᵗʰ: 1 Midshipman & 20 Men cleard ¾ of a Mile

5ᵗʰ: continued working on the Roads

6ᵗʰ: Compleated the new Road & Return'd to Camp.

7ᵗʰ: Sʳ P. Halkets Brigade March'd with

[35] The Gordon Journal: "This morning an Engineer and 100 men   . ."

[36] The only hint given in the Gordon Journal as to the author of the original document is under this date. The Gordon Journal reads, "Mr. Spendlowe and self with 20 of our men went to the place where the new road comes into the old one.   . ." "Self" here seems to refer to "Midshipman"; but Mr. Gordon often refers to himself as an engineer and never once inserts his own name, though he was a most important official. Gordon probably accompanied or followed Spendlowe.

2 Field Pieces and some Waggons with Provisions 1 Midshipman & 12 Seamen were Orderd to Afsist the Train June 9th. Inactive June 10th: The General March'd wth. the remaining part of the Army.

25th: it was reported that a party of Indians had Surprized Kill'd, and Scalp'd 2 families to the Number of 12 within 4 Miles of ye Fort

June 26th: Accounts of another family's Scalp'd within 3 Miles of us. The Governor detach'd a party to bury the Dead, and to look for the Indians, they found a Child standing in the Water scalp'd, which had 2 holes in its Skull, they brought it to the Doctor, who drefsed it but Died in a Week.[37]

June 10th: the last Division of His Majesty's Forces March'd from *Wills Creek* with General Braddock, when the General Arrived at the little Meadows 22 Miles from the *Creek*, and having all his Forces wth. him, found that the Carriages, Pack

[37] Entries written by one while detained at Fort Cumberland. If written by Gordon he hastened immediately to the front, for he was with Braddock's advance on July 9.

horses &cᵃ. he had with him, retardid his
Marches greatly, insomuch that in all prob-
ability, the French would be renforced,
before he could poſsibly get there, provided
he kept the whole Army together — he
therefore selected 1200 of the Choicest Men
besides Artillery & Seamen with the most
Neceſsary Stores that might be wanted,
which compleated 51 Carriages, and left
the heavy Baggage Provisions &cᵃ. with
Colᵒ. Dunbar and the rest of the Forces wᵗʰ.
Orders to follow as fast as poſsible: then
March'd & continued untill 8ᵗʰ. July without Interruption save 8 or 9 Scalps on the
March a Number much inferior to the
Expectations, he Encamp'd within 8 Miles
of *Fort Dec Quisne* where he held a Councill
of War, when it was unaimously agreed
that they should paſs the *Monongohela* River
in the Morning twice and that the advanced
Party should March at 2 o'Clock in the
Morning to secure that paſs (the River
being very broad and easily defended as
the Fort was very near they thought it
advisable to take that oppertunity, that the
Enemy might not have a View of them,
Therefore the General order'd that the

Army should March over with fixt Bayonets
to make a show.

On the 9th. July the advanced party of
400 Men March'd about 7. o'Clock some
Indians Rush'd out of the Bushes, but did
no Execution, the Party went on & secured
both pafses of the River, and at 11 the
Main Body began to crofs with Colours
flying, Drums beating, & Fifes playing the
Granadier's March, and soon formed, when
they thought that the French would not
Attack them, as they might have done it
wth. such advantages in crofsing the *Monongohela*, The advanc'd party was ¼ Mile
before the Main Body, the Rear of which
was just over the River, when the Front
was attack'd The 2. Granadier Compys.
formed the Flank The Piquets with the
rest of the Men were Sustaining the Carpenters while they were cutting the Roads.
The first Fire the Enemy gave was in
Front, & they likewise gaul'd the Piquets
in Flank, so that in few Minutes the Grana-
diers were nearly cut to pieces and drove
into the greatest Confusion as was Capt.
Polsons Compy. of Carpentrs. As soon as
the Main Body heard that the Front was

Attack'd they instantly advanced to secure
them but found them retreating Upon
which, the General Orderd the Artillery
to draw up, & the Battalion to form, by
this time the Enemy had Attack'd the
Main Body, which faced to the Right &
left and engaged them, but could not see
whom they Fired at, it was in an open
Road, that the Main Body were drawn up,
but the Trees were excefsive thick round
them, And the Enemy had pofsefsion of a
Hill to the Right, which consequently was
a great advantage to them, Many Officers
declare, that they never saw above 5 of the
Enemy at one time during the whole Action
Our Soldiers were Encouraged to make
many Attempts by the Officers (who be-
haved Gloriously) to take the Hill, but they
had been so intimidated before by seeing
their Comrades Scalp'd in their sight and
such Numbers falling, that as they advanced up towards the Hill and there
Officer's being pict off which was generally
the Case; they turn'd to their R^t. About &
retired down the Hill.   When the General
perceived & was convinced that the Soldiers
would not fight in a regular Manner with-

out Officers, he devided them into small parties, and endeavour'd to surround the Enemy, but by this time the Major part of the Officers were either Kill'd or Wounded, and in short the Soldiers were totally deaf to the Commands & persuasions of the few Officers that were left unhurt. The General had 4 Horses shot under him before he was wounded, which was towards the latter part of the Action, when he was put into a Waggon with great dificulty as he was very Sollicitious for being left in the Field. The Retreat now became general, and it was the opinion of many people that had we greater Numbers, it would have been just the same thing, as our advanc'd party never regained the Ground they were first Attack'd upon, it was extreamly lucky they pursued no farther than the first Crofsing the River but they kill'd & Scalp'd every one they met with, The Army March'd all Night & Join'd Colonel Dunbar the next Day, 50 Miles distance from the Field of Battle, when the General order'd Colº. Dunbar to prepare for a Retreat in Order for which, they were Obliged to destroy great quantities of

Stores and Provisions, to furnish the Wounded Officers & Soldiers with Waggons The Generals Pains encreased hourly, and on the 12th of July he Died greatly lamented by the whole Army, was decently though privately buried the next Morning.

The Numbers kill'd; Wounded & left in the Field as appeared by the Returns of the different Companies were 896 besides Officers The 2 Companies of the Grenadiers and Carpenters sufferd most Col^o. Dunbars Grenadiers were 79 Compleat out of which 9 Returned untouch'd. Sr P. Halkets, were 69 & only 13 came out of ye Field Every Grenadier Officer was either kill'd or Wounded The Seamen had 11 Kill'd & wounded out of 33 it was impoſsible to tell the exact Nunbers of the Enemy but it was premised by the continual smart Fire the kept during the whole Action, that they must have at least Man for Man M^r. Engineer Gordon [38] was the first Man that saw the Enemy, being in the

---

[38] The Gordon Journal: "One of our Engineers, who was in front of the Carpenters marking the road, saw the Enemy first." Who but Gordon would have omitted his name under these circumstances?

Front of the Carpenters, making & Picketing the Roads for them, and he declared where he first descover'd them, that they were on the Run, which plainly shews they were just come from *Fort Dec Quesne* and that their principal Intention was to secure the pafs of *Monnongohela River* but the Officer who was their leader, drefsed like an Indian, wth. a Gorgeton, waved his Hatt, by way of Signal to disperse to ye Right and left forming a half Moon Col^o. Dunbar continued his Retreat and Arrived with the Remains of the Army at *Fort Cumberland* the 20th. July, and the 21st. the Wounded Officers & Soldiers were brought in. . . . 30th. July Orders were given for the Army to March the 2nd. August 1st. August Col^o. Dunbar received a Letter from Commodore Kepple to send the Seamen to *Hampton* and accordingly the 2^d. they March'd with the Army & on the 3^d. August left them August 5th. Arrived at *Winchester* August 11th. March'd into *Fredericksburgh* and hired a Vefsel to carry the Seamen to *Hampton* where they embarked on board his Majesty's Ship Guarland the 18th. August 1755.

4: 6 pounders. 2. 12 pounders, 3 Howitzers, 8 Cohorns, 51 Carriages of Provisions Ammunition Hospital Stores, The Generals private Chest which had about 1000£ in it with 200 Horses loaded with Officers Baggage [39]

[39] This last paragraph is evidently an additional memorandum of British loss. The contents of the chest was undoubtedly £10,000.

CHAPTER V

THE BATTLE OF THE MONONGAHELA

SIR PETER HALKET moved out from Fort Cumberland on June 7 with a brigade comprising the 44th Regiment, two Independent Companies of New York, two companies of Virginia Rangers, one of Maryland Rangers, a total of nine hundred and eighty-four men, six hundred woodchoppers under Sir John St. Clair having been sent forward to widen and improve Washington's road. The next day but one Colonel Thomas Dunbar marched away with another brigade comprising the 48th Regiment, a company of carpenters, three companies of Virginia Rangers, and one from South and North Carolina each, a total of nine hundred and ninety-three men. On the tenth, Braddock and his aides and the rest of the army which was approximately two thousand two hundred strong — a force powerful enough to have razed Duquesne, Venango, La Bœuf, Presque Isle, and Niagara to the ground — if it could have reached them.

This Franklin who secured Braddock horses and wagons was a prophet. And once he predicted that this " slender line " of an army would be greatly in danger of Indian ambuscade " and be cut, like a thread, into several pieces, which, from their distance, cannot come up in time to support each other." Braddock laughed at the prophecy, but his army had not been swallowed up in the gloom of the forests two days before its line was thinner and longer than Braddock could ever have believed. When encamped at night, the line of wagons compactly drawn together was half a mile long; in marching order by day the army was often spread out to a length of four miles. And even in this fashion it could only creep along. Halket with the first division made only five miles in three days. In ten days Braddock had only covered the twenty-four miles to Little Crossings. The road makers followed implicitly the Indian path where it was possible; when on the high ground the road

was so rugged that many wagons were
entirely demolished and more temporarily
disabled; when off this track in the ravines
they were buried axle deep in the bogs.

To haul the wagons and cannon over this
worst road ever trod Braddock had the poor-
est horses available. All the weak, spav-
ined, wind-broken, and crippled beasts in
Pennsylvania, Maryland, and Virginia were
palmed off on Braddock by unscrupulous
contractors. And horses, dead or dying,
were always left with the demolished
wagons. "There has been vile manage-
ment in regard to horses," wrote Washington; before the army had covered one third
of its journey there were not enough to
draw all the wagons, the strongest being
sent back each day to bring up the wagons
left behind the morning before. The con-
tinuous diet of salt meat brought an
epidemic of bloody flux on the army; some
died, many were sick. Washington's strong
system was in the grasp of a fever before
Little Crossings was reached.

The situation now was desperate and
would have appalled a less stubborn man
than Edward Braddock. Acting on Wash-

ington's advice he here divided his army, preparing to push on to Fort Duquesne with a flying column of fourteen hundred men. Washington found the first western river almost dry and reasoned that Riviere aux Bœufs would be too dry to transport southward the reinforcements that were hurrying from Canada.

On the nineteenth, Braddock advanced with Colonel Halket and Lieutenant Colonels Burton and Gage and Major Sparks, leaving Colonel Dunbar and Major Chapman — to their disgust — to hobble on with the sick and dying men and horses, the sorry line of wagons creaking under their heavy loads. The young Virginian Colonel was left at the very first camp in a raging fever. Though unable to push on further with the column that would capture Duquesne, yet Braddock considerately satisfied the ambition of Washington by promising that he should be brought up before the attack was made. Washington wrote home that he would not miss the capture of Duquesne " for five hundred pounds! "

With the flying column were taken the Indians that were with the army but which numbered less than a dozen. Braddock has been severely blamed for his neglect of the Indians, but any earnest study of this campaign will assure the student that the commanding general was no more at fault here than for the failure of the contractors and the indifference of the colonies. He had been promised Indians as freely as stores and horses and wagons. The Indian question seems to have been handled most wretchedly since Washington's late campaign. Through the negligence of the busy-body Dinwiddie (so eager for so many unimportant matters) even the majority of the Indians who served Washington faithfully and had followed his retreating army back to Virginia were allowed to drift back to the French through sheer neglect. As none of Dinwiddie's promises were fulfilled in this respect Braddock turned in despair to Morris for such Ohio Indians as were living in Pennsylvania. There had been at least three hundred Indians of the Six Nations living in that province, but in April the Pennsylvania Assembly had resolved to " do nothing more for them "; accordingly they went westward and most

of them joined the French.   Morris, however, urged George Croghan to send word
to the Delawares, Shawanese, Wyandots,
etc., bidding them come and join Braddock's army.   But Croghan brought less
than fifty and Braddock was not destined to
keep all of these, for Colonel Innes, commanding at Fort Cumberland, not desiring
the Indian families on his hands during the
absence of the fathers, persuaded Braddock
that there were not enough to add to the
fighting strength of the army and that a
few would be as serviceable for spies as
many.   Nor was this bad reasoning: Braddock would have been no better off with
thirty than with ten.   The fact is, he was
in nothing deceived more by false promises
and assurances than in the matter of Indian
coöperation.   And was he more at fault
for the lack of frontiersmen?   True, he
refused the services of Captain Jack and his
company, but only because the latter
refused to be governed by the discipline to
which the rest of the army was subject;
Braddock could not agree to such an
arrangement and it is doubtful if Washington would have acted differently under

similar circumstances. At least the Virginian had nothing to do with Captain Jack's renowned company the year before. To other border fighters Braddock gave a warm reception; Gist and Croghan, the two best known men on the frontier, held important offices in the army. It is as easy as common to lay at the door of a defeated and dead commander all the misfortunes of a campaign; whatever Braddock's errors, the fact remains that the colonies failed absolutely to make the least move to provide an Indian army for Braddock's use. Nothing could have more surely promised defeat and disgrace.

The flying column flew like a partridge with a broken wing. " We set out," wrote Washington who started with it but was compelled to stop, " with less than thirty carriages, including those that transported the ammunition for the howitzers, and six-pounders, and all of them strongly horsed; which was a prospect that conveyed infinite delight to my mind, though I was excessively ill at the time. But this prospect was soon clouded, and my hopes brought very low indeed, when I found, that,

instead of pushing on with vigor, without
regarding a little rough road, they were
halting to level every mole-hill, and to
erect bridges over every brook, by which
means we were four days in getting twelve
miles.''

On the third of July the flying column
had passed the Youghiogheny and were
encamped ten miles north of it, forty miles
from Fort Duquesne. It had not averaged
three miles a day since leaving Little
Crossings! Here a Council of War was
held to decide whether to push on alone
or await the coming of Dunbar and the
wagons. Could the Grenadiers and their
officers have seen through that narrow path
to their destination, how quickly would
their decision have been made, how eagerly
would they have hurried on to the Ohio!
Contrecœur at Fort Duquesne was in a
miserable plight; every returning red-skin
told of the advance of the great British
army in the face of Governor Duquesne's
proud boast to Vaudreuil that it was impossible for the English to cross the Alleghenies in sufficient force to cause uneasi-
ness! Braddock, despite the utter lack of

proper support from the colonies, was accomplishing the eighth wonder of the world. It was desperate work. But a Bull-dog was creeping nearer each day.

Throughout the winter the British ministry and the Court of Versailles had been exchanging the most ridiculous pretenses of peace while secretly preparing for war with dispatch. For every ill-recruited regiment King George sent to Virginia, King Louis sent two famous regiments to Canada, and they arrived there despite Boscawen, the English admiral, who captured two unimportant ships. Yet that was enough to precipitate the struggle and save more fables from the respective ambassadors; "I will not pardon the piracies of that insolent nation," exclaimed Louis — and open war was inevitable.

At his landing at Quebec Vaudreuil found not less than twelve thousand soldiers in Canada to defend the claims of his King. But that was a long frontier to man, from Quebec to New Orleans, and in April only about one thousand men were forwarded to defend the Ohio river. Of these Contrecœur had not more than three hundred, probably less.   The summer before he had two thousand defenders, but Duquesne, blindly trusting to the ephemeral league he had made with the Alleghenies, had not been liberal again.   In vain Contrecœur sent messages northward to Venango and Presque Isle.   Riviere aux Bœufs was as dry as the Youghiogheny.   Inevitable surrender or capitulation stared the French commander in the face.   Even the crowds of Indians within hail were not to be reckoned on; they were terrified at the proportions of Braddock's army.

Accordingly, Contrecœur made his arrangements for a capitulation, as Washington had done one year ago.   Braddock had accomplished the impossible; the Indians were demoralized and took to " cooking and counciling "; Fort Duquesne was as good as captured.

On the seventh Braddock reached Brush Fork of Turtle Creek, but the country immediately between him and the Ohio was so rough that the army turned westward and pitched its nineteenth encampment in Long Run valley two miles from the Monongahela.   Here Washington came up

with the army in a covered wagon, still
weak but ready to move with the army in
the morning and sleep in Duquesne that
night. The whole army was infused with
this hope as the ninth of July dawned.

For no one questioned Braddock's success
if he could once throw that army across the
mountains. No one knew the situation
better than Washington, and early in the
campaign he wrote his brother: " As to
any danger from the enemy, I look upon
it as trifling." In London profane wits
cited Scripture (Ezekiel xxxv: 1–10) to
justify the conquest of the Ohio valley:
" Moreover, the word of the Lord came
unto me saying, Son of man, set thy face
against Mount Seir and prophesy against it,
and say unto it, thus saith the Lord God:
Behold, O mount Seir, I am against thee
and I will stretch out mine hand against
thee and I will make thee most deso-
late. . . . Because thou hast said,
These two nations and these two countries
shall be mine, and we will possess it."
Already subscription papers were being
passed about in Philadelphia to provide
festal fires to illumine the Quaker City

when the news of Braddock's victory came.

"Why, the d—l," exclaimed one of the enthusiasts to that odd man Franklin who did not sign his name at once, "you surely don't suppose the fort will not be taken?" "I don't know it will not be taken," replied the Postmaster-General, "but I know that the events of war are subject to great uncertainty." A jingling ballad in Chester County, Pennsylvania, was spreading throughout the frontier. It ran, in part:

> To arms, to arms! my jolly grenadiers!
>   Hark, how the drums do roll it along!
> To horse, to horse, with valiant good cheer;
>   We'll meet our proud foe, before it is long.
>   Let not your courage fail you:
>   Be valiant, stout and bold;
>   And it will soon avail you,
>   My loyal hearts of gold.
> Huzzah, my valiant countrymen! — again I say
>   huzzah!
> 'Tis nobly done — the day's our own — huzzah,
>   huzzah!
>
> March on, march on, brave Braddock leads
>   the foremost;
>   The battle is begun as you may fairly see.
> Stand firm, be bold, and it will soon be over;

We'll soon gain the field from our proud
    enemy.
      A squadron now appears, my boys;
        If that they do but stand!
      Boys, never fear, be sure you mind
        The word of command!
Huzzah, my valiant countrymen! — again I say
    huzzah!
'Tis nobly done — the day's our own — huzzah,
    huzzah!

Before daybreak on the morning of the
fatal ninth Lieutenant Colonel Gage moved
to the Monongahela to secure the two fords
the army was to use on the last day's
march. At four o'clock Sir John St. Clair
with two hundred and fifty men went forward to prepare the roads. At five Braddock
advanced and made the first crossing at
eight o'clock. He then formed his army
for a triumphant march to the second ford
and on to Fort Duquesne. It had been
feared that, however weak, Contrecœur
would attempt to defend this ford of the
Monongahela. But this fear was dissipated
on receipt of the news that Gage held the
second ford.

Contrecœur knew it would be foolhardy

to give Braddock battle. He was in no mind to waste his men futilely. He knew an honorable capitulation was all for which he could hope. But on the 8th a captain of the regulars, M. de Beaujeu, asked leave to go out with a band to oppose Braddock's passage of the Monongahela. Reluctantly, it is said, Contrecœur gave his permission and, the whole garrison desiring to attend Beaujeu, the commander detailed him selected troops on the condition that he could obtain the assistance of the Indians who were about the fort.

The impetuous Beaujeu hurried off to the Indians and unfolded his plan to them. But they were afraid of Braddock; some of them had even gone into the English camp, at Cumberland, or in the mountains, on pretense of joining the English army; they had seen the long lines of grenadiers and wagons laden with cannon.

" How, my Father," they replied, " are you so bent upon death that you would also sacrifice us? With our eight hundred men do you ask us to attack four thousand English? Truly, this is not the saying of a wise man. But we will lay up what we have heard, and tomorrow you shall know our thoughts.''

Baffled, Beaujeu withdrew while the redskinned allies of the French frittered away the hours in debate — and the spies brought word that Braddock was encamped in Long Run valley. The indomitable Beaujeu, however, went and examined the ground at the ford of the Monongahela, which Braddock would pass on the next day. On the ninth, however, the Indians brought word that they would not join in the unequal contest.

But even as they spoke an Indian scout came running down the narrow trail toward the fort. He brought the news of Braddock's advance on the Monongahela fords. Beaujeu, cunning actor, played his last card desperately and well:

'' I am determined,'' he cried, '' to go out against the enemy; I am certain of victory. What! will you suffer your father to depart alone?''

The reproach stung the savage breasts. In a moment hundreds of hoarse voices were drowning the long roll of the drums. A mad scene followed; wild with enthusi-

asm, casks of bullets and flints and powder
were rolled to fort gates and their heads
knocked out.   About these the savages,
even while painting themselves for the
fray, came in crowds, each one free to help
himself as he needed.   Then came the
race for the ford of the Monongahela.
Down the narrow trail burst the horde of
warriors, led by the daring Beaujeu dressed
in savage costume, an Indian gorget swing-
ing from his neck for good fortune.   Behind
him poured Delawares, Ojibways, Pottaw-
attamies, Abenakis, Caughnawagas, Iroquois, Ottawas, led by their young King
Pontiac; Shawanese, Wyandots, Hurons,
led by Athanasius from the mission of
Lorette, who gloried in a name " torn from
the most famous page of Christian history."
With the six hundred savages ran two
hundred Canadians and four score French
regulars.

This rabble could not have left Fort
Duquesne before high noon; no wonder
Beaujeu ran — fearing Braddock had passed
the battle-ground he had chosen last night.
In that case he despaired of delaying the
advance even a single day; yet in one day

the expected reinforcements might arrive from the north!

Washington rode with Braddock today, though he rode on a pillow in his saddle. In after life he often recalled the sight of Braddock's grenadiers marching beside the Monongahela in battle array, a fine picture with the thin red line framed in the fresh green of the forests. With the receipt of Gage's note, the fear of ambuscade which had been omnipresent since the army left Fort Cumberland, vanished. During that month the Indian guides, flanking squads, and woodchoppers had rushed into camp time and again calling the companies to arms; each alarm had been false. As Fort Duquesne was neared Braddock grew doubly cautious. He even attempted to leave the Indian trail which ran through the " Narrows " and which crossed the Monongahela at the mouth of Turtle Creek. When another course was found impossible for the wagons he turned reluctantly back to the old thoroughfare, but had passed the " Narrows " safely and his advance guards now held the fords. All was well.

By two o'clock Braddock was across the

river, bag and baggage.   Beyond, the Indian trail wound along to the uplands,
skirting the heads of numerous ravines and
clinging persistently, like all the trails of
the Indians and buffalo, to the high ground
between the brook and swamp.   The ridge
which the trail followed here to the second
terrace was twenty rods in width, with the
path near the center.   On the west a deep
ravine, completely hidden in the deep
underbrush, lay almost parallel with the
trail for a distance of over five hundred
feet.   On the opposite side smaller ravines
also lay nearly parallel with the trail.   On
the high ground between these hidden
ravines, and not more than two hundred
feet from them, Braddock's engineers and
woodchoppers widened their road for Gage's
advance guard which was ordered to march
on until three o'clock.

As the engineers reached the extremity
of the second terrace Beaujeu came bound-
ing into sight, the pack of eight hundred
wolves at his heels.   Seeing the English,
the daring but dismayed Frenchman
stopped still in his tracks.   He was an hour
too late.   Attempting to surprise Brad-

dock, Beaujeu was himself surprised. But he waved his hat above his head and the crowd of warriors scattered behind him like a partridge's brood into the forest leaves.

The French captain knew the ground and Braddock did not, and the ground was admirably formed for a desperate stand against the advancing army. Burton, who was just leaving the river shore, was ordered up to support Gage on the second upland after the first fire. This brought the whole army, save four hundred men, to the second terrace between the unseen ravines on the east and west. Into these ravines poured the Indian rabble. The ravine on the east being shorter than that on the west, many savages ran through it and posted themselves in the dense under-brush on the hillside.

Thus, in a twinkling of an eye, the Indians running southward in the two ravines and the British northward on the high ground between them, the fatal position of the battle was quickly assumed.[40]

[40] *British Newspaper Accounts of Braddock's Defeat*, p. 10. Pennsylvania *Colonial Records*, vol. vi., p. 482.

No encounter has been more incorrectly described and pictured than the Battle of the Monongahela.[41]   Braddock was not surprised; his advance guard saw the enemy long before they opened fire; George Croghan affirmed that the grenadiers delivered their first charge when two hundred yards distant from the Indians, completely throwing it away.   Nor did Braddock march blindly into a deep ravine; his army was ever on the high ground, caught almost in the vortex of the cross-fire of the savages hidden on the brink of the ravines on either side, or posted on the high ground to the right.[42]

The road was but twelve feet in width. Even as Burton came up, Gage's grenadiers were frightened and retreating.   The meeting of the advancing and retiring troops caused a fatal confusion and delay in the narrow road.   The fire from the Indians on the high ground to the right being severe, Braddock attempted to form his bewildered men and charge.   It was

[41] This view of Braddock's defeat is given in the late John Fiske's recent volume, *New France and New England.*

[42] London *Public Advertiser*, November 3, 1755.

futile. The companies were in an inextricable tangle. Finally, to reduce things to order, the various standards were advanced in different directions and the officers strove to organize their commands in separate detachments, with a hope of surrounding the savages. This, too, proved futile. The Indians on either side completely hidden in the ravines, the smoke of the rifles hardly visible through the dense underbrush, poured a deadly fire on the swarm of red-coats huddled in the narrow track. Not a rifle ball could miss its mark there. As the standards were advanced here and there, the standard bearers and the officers who followed encouraging their men to form again were shot down both from behind and before.[43] As once and again the paralyzed grenadiers broke into the forest to raid the ravines, in the vain hope of dislodging the enemy, they offered only a surer mark for the thirsty rifles toward which they ran.

The Virginians took to the trees like ducks to water, but the sight enraged Braddock, mad to have the men form in battle

[43] London *Public Advertiser*, November 3, 1755.

line and charge in solid phalanx.   In vain
Washington pleaded to be allowed to place
his men behind the trees; Braddock drove
them away with the flat blade of his sword.
Yet they came back and fought bravely
from the trees as was their habit.   But it
availed nothing to fight behind trees with
the enemy on both flanks; the Virginians
were, after all, no safer there than elsewhere, as the death-roll plainly shows.
The provincial portion of the army suffered
as heavily, if not more heavily, than any
other.   No army could have stood its
ground there and won that battle.   The
only chance of victory was to advance or
retreat out of range of those hidden rifles.
The army could not be advanced for every
step brought the men nearer the very center of that terrible cross-fire.   And the
Bull-dog Braddock knew not the word
" retreat."   That was the secret of his
defeat.[44]

Soon there were not enough officers left
to command the men, most of whom were

[44] Cf. *British Newspaper Accounts of Braddock's
Defeat*, p. 9.   Pennsylvania *Colonial Records*, vol. vi.,
p. 482.   London *Public Advertiser*, November 3, 1755.

hopelessly bewildered at seeing half the army shot down, by a foe they themselves had never seen. Many survivors of the battle affirmed that they never saw above five Indians during the conflict. Braddock was mortally wounded by a ball which pierced his right arm and lung. Sir Peter Halket lay dead, his son's dead corpse lying across his own. Of twenty-one captains, seven were dead and seven wounded; of thirty-eight lieutenants, fifteen were wounded and eleven were dead; of fourteen second lieutenants or ensigns, five were wounded and three were dead; of fifty-eight sergeants, twenty were wounded and seventeen dead; of sixty-one corporals and bombardiers, twenty-two were wounded and eighteen dead; of eighteen gunners, eight were wounded and six were dead; of twelve hundred privates, three hundred and twenty-eight were wounded and three hundred and eighty-six were dead. Each Frenchman, Canadian, and Indian had hit his man and more than every other one had killed his man. Their own absolutely impregnable position can be realized when it is known that not twenty-five French,

Canadians or Indians were killed and wounded. Among the first to fall was the hero of the day, Beaujeu; his Indian gorget could not save his own life, but it delayed the capture of Fort Duquesne — three years.

Yet the stubborn, doomed army held its ground until the retreat was ordered. The wounded Braddock, who pleaded, it is said, to be left upon the ground, and even begged for Croghan's pistol with which to finish what a French bullet had begun, was placed in a cart and afterwards in a wagon and brought off the field.[45] No sooner was retreat ordered than it became an utter rout. Some fifty Indians pursued the army into the river, but none crossed it. Here and there efforts were made to stem the tide but to no purpose. The army fled back to Dunbar, who had now crawled along to Laurel Hill and was encamped at a great spring at the foot of what is now Dunbar's Knob, half a mile north of Jumonville's hiding place and grave. Dunbar's situation was already deplorable, even

[45] Cf. *British Newspaper Accounts of Braddock's Defeat*, p. 9; London *Public Advertiser*, November 3, 1755.

Washington having prophesied that, though he had crossed the worst of the mountain road, he could never reach Fort Duquesne.

But as Braddock's demoralized army threw itself upon him, Dunbar's condition was indescribably wretched. A large portion of the survivors of the battle and of Dunbar's own command, lost to all order, hurried on toward Fort Cumberland. Dunbar himself, now senior officer in command, ordered his cannons spiked and his ammunition destroyed and, with such horses as could be of service, began to retreat across the mountains. For this he was, and has often been, roundly condemned; yet, since we have Washington's plain testimony that he could never have hauled his wagons and cannon over the thirty comparatively easy miles to Fort Duquesne, who can fairly blame him for not attempting to haul them over the sixty difficult miles to Fort Cumberland? To fortify himself, so far removed from hopes of sustenance and succor, was equally impossible. There was nothing Dunbar could do but retreat.

The dying Braddock, tumbling about in a covered wagon on the rough road, spoke little to the few men who remained faithfully beside him. Only once or twice in the three days he lived did he speak of the battle; and then he only sighed to himself softly: "Who would have thought it?" Once, turning to the wounded Orme, he said: "We shall better know how to deal with them another time." During his last hours Braddock seems to have regarded his young Virginian aide, Washington, whose advice he had followed only indifferently throughout the campaign, with utmost favor, bequeathing him his favorite charger and his servant. On the night of the twelfth of July, in a camp in an Indian orchard, near what is now Braddock's Run, a mile and more east of Fort Necessity, in Great Meadows, Edward Braddock died. In the morning he was buried in the center of the roadway. Undoubtedly Washington read the service over the Briton's grave. When the army marched eastward it pased over the grave, obliterating its site from even an Indian's keen eye. In 1823, when the Braddock's Road was

being repaired, what were undoubtedly his
bones were uncovered, together with military trappings, etc.   These were placed in
the dry ground above the neighboring run,
the spot being now marked by solemn
pines.

Whatever Braddock's faults and foibles,
he accomplished a great feat in leading a
comparatively powerful army across the
Alleghenies, and had he been decently
supported by the colonies, there would
have been no doubt of his success.   As it
was, shamefully hampered and delayed by
the procrastinating indifference of the
colonies, deceived and defrauded by wolf-
ish contractors, abandoned by the Indians
because of the previous neglect of the
Colonial governors and assemblies, never-
theless the campaign was a distinct success,
until at the last moment, Fate capriciously
dashed the chalice from Braddock's lips.

The shattered army reached Fort Cumberland on July 20.   The tale of disaster
had preceded it.   The festal fires were
not kindled in Philadelphia.   Now, for the
first time the colonies were awakened to
the true situation, and in the months

following paid dearly for their supine indifference.

For with Beaujeu's victory the French arms became impregnable on the Ohio. Braddock's defeat brought ten-fold more wretchedness than his victory could ever have brought of advantage. After that terrible scene of savagery at Fort Duquesne on the night of the victory, when the few prisoners taken were burned at the stake, there were no wavering Indians. And instantly the frontier was overrun with marauding bands which drove back to the inhabited parts of the country every advanced settlement. All the Virginian outposts were driven in; and even the brave Moravian missionaries in Pennsylvania and New York gave up their work before the red tide of war which now set eastward upon the long frontiers.

For Shirley had likewise been beaten back from Fort Niagara, and Johnson had not captured Fort Crown Point. Two of the campaigns of 1755 were utter failures.

CHAPTER VI

A DESCRIPTION OF THE BACKWOODS

THE clearest insight into the days when Braddock's Road was built, and the most vivid pictures of the country through which it wound its course, are given in certain letters of a British officer who accompanied Braddock. No treatise on Braddock's expedition could be in any measure complete without reproducing this amusing, interesting, yet pitiful testimony to the difficulties experienced by these first English officers to enter the backwoods of America. This is given in a volume entitled *Extracts of Letters from an officer in one of those Regiments to his friend in London*, published in London in the year of Braddock's Defeat:

"You desire me to let you know the Particulars of our Expedition, and an Account at large of the Nature of the Country, and how they live here; also of

the Manner of the Service, and which
Corps is the most agreeable to serve in,
because it has been proposed to you to
strive to buy a Commission here, and that
you awaited my Advice to determine.
Dear Sir, I love you so well that I shall at
once tell you, I reckon the Day I bought
my Commission the most unhappy in my
Life, excepting that in which I landed in
this Country. As for the Climate, it is
excessive hot in Summer, and as disagree-
ably cold in Winter, and there is no Comfort in the Spring; none of those Months
of gentle genial Warmth, which revives all
Nature, and fills every Soul with vernal
Delight; far from this, the Spring here is
of very few Days, for as soon as the severe
Frosts go off, the Heat of the neighbouring
Sun brings on Summer at once, one Day
shall be Frost, and the next more scorching
or sultry and faint than the hottest Dog-
Day in *England*. What is excessively disagreeable here is, that the Wealth of the
Country consists in Slaves, so that all one
eats rises out of driving and whipping these
poor Wretches; this Kind of Authority so
Corrupts the Mind of the Masters, and

makes them so overbearing, that they are
the most troublesome Company upon Earth,
which adds much to the Uncomfortableness
of the Place. You cannot conceive how it
strikes the Mind on the first Arrival, to
have all these black Faces with grim Looks
round you, instead of being served by
blooming Maid Servants, or genteel white
Livery Men: I was invited to Supper by a
rich Planter, and the Heat of the Climate,
the dim Light of the Myrtle Wax-Candles,
and the Number of black half-naked Servants that attended us, made me think of
the infernal Regions, and that I was at
Supper with *Pluto*, only there was no beautiful *Proserpine*, for the Lady of the House
was more like one of the Furies; she had
passed through the Education of the College of *Newgate*, as great Numbers from
thence arrive here yearly; Most being cunning Jades, some pick up foolish Planters;
this Lady's Husband was far from a Fool,
but had married, not only for the Charms
of her Person, but because her Art and
Skill was Quite useful to him in carrying
on his Business and Affairs, many of which
were worthy of an adept in the College she

came from.   Among others he made me
pay for my Supper by selling me a Horse
upon Honour, which, as soon as it was cool,
shewed itself Dog-lame and Moon-blind.

" As for eating, they have the Names of
almost every Thing that is delicious, or in
Fashion in *England*, but they give them to
Things as little like as *Cæsar* or *Pompey*
were to the *Negroes* whom they call by
those *Names*.   For what they call a Hare
is a Creature half Cat, half Rabbet, with
white strong Flesh, and that burrows in
rotten Trees; they call a Bird not much
bigger than a Fieldfare, with hard, dry,
strong Flesh, hardly eatable, a Partridge.
The best Thing they have is a wild Turky,
but this is only in Season one Month in the
Year; the rest it is hard, strong, and dry.
As for Beef, the Months of *October* and
November excepted, it is Carrion; that is to
say, so lean as it would not be called Meat
in *England*; their Mutton is always as
strong Goats' Flesh; their Veal is red and
lean, and indeed the Heat of the Summer
and the pinching Frost of Winter, makes
all like *Pharaoh's* lean Kine.   They brag of
the Fruits, that they have such plenty of

Peaches as to feed Hogs; and indeed that
is true, they are fit for nothing else; I do
not remember, among the Multitudes I
have tasted, above one or two that were
eatable, the rest were either mealy or
choaky. Melons grow in Fields, and are
plentier than Pumpkins in *England*, as large
and as tasteless; there are such Quantities
that the Houses stink of them; the Heat of
the Country makes them at once mellow,
so that they hardly ever have the fine racy
Taste of an *English* good Melon, for in
England you have many bad Melons to
one good; but here the Heat makes all
Fruits like us young fellows, rotten before
they are ripe. With respect to Fish, they
have neither Salmon, Carp, Trout, Smelts,
nor hardly any one good Kind of Fish.
They give the Name of Trout to a white
Sea-fish, no more like a Trout than a Cat
to a Hare; they have one good, nay excellent Kind of Fish, I mean a Turtle; but as
Scarce as in *England*. With respect to
public Diversions, the worst *English* Country Town exceeds all they have in the
whole Province. As to Drink, *Burgundy*
and *Champaign* were scarce ever heard of;

Claret they have but poor Stuff, tawny and prick'd, for it cannot stand the Heat of the Summer, which also spoils the *Port*; the *Madeira* is the best Wine they have, but that only of the worst Growths, for the best are sent to *Jamaica* or *England*; their only tolerable Drink is Rum Punch, which they swill Morning, Noon, and Night. Their Produce is Tobacco; they are so attached to that, and their Avarice to raise it, makes them neglect every Comfort of Life; But the Intemperance of the Climate affects not only all the Cattle, Fruits, and Growths of the Country, but the human Race; and it is rare to see a native reach 50 Years of Age. I have heard from the best Judges, I mean the kind hearted Ladies most in Vogue, that a *Virginian* is old at 30, as an *Englishman* is at 60. The Ladies I speak of are well experienced, and for most of them the Public have for peculiar Merit paid the Passage, and honoured with an Order for Transportation on Record. I would not deceive you so have told you the truth; I have not exaggerated, but have omitted many disagreeable Circumstances, such as Thunder Storms,

Yellow Fevers, Musketoes, other Vermin, &c with which I shall not trouble you. The Ship is just going."

.   .   .   .   .   .

" I Sent a Letter to you by Captain *Johnson* bound for *Bristol*, with a full Account of the Country, by which you will see the Reasons why it will be highly improper for you to buy into the Troops here; I send this by a Ship bound for *London*.

" They make here a Division between the Settlements and the Woods, though the Settlements are what we should call very woody in *Europe*. The Face of the Country is entirely different from any Thing I ever saw before; the Fields have not the Appearance of what bears that Name in *Europe*, instead of ploughed Grounds or Meadows, they are all laid out in Hillocks, each of which bears Tobacco Plants, with Paths hoed between. When the Tobacco is green it looks like a Coppice; when pulled the Ground looks more like Hop-Yards than Fields, which makes a very disagreeable Appearance to the Eye. The Indian Corn also, and all their Culture runs upon hilling with the Hoe, and the *Indian*

Corn grows like Reeds to eight or nine
Feet high. Indeed in some Parts of the
Country Wheat grows, but Tobacco and
Indian Corn is the chief.

" From the Heart of the Settlements we
are now got into the Cow-Pens, the Keepers
of these are very extraordinary Kind of
Fellows, they drive up their Herds on
Horseback, and they had need do so, for
their Cattle are near as wild as Deer; a
Cow-Pen generally consists of a very large
Cottage or House in the Woods, with about
four-score or one hundred Acres, inclosed
with high Rails and divided; a small In-
closure they keep for Corn, for the Family,
the rest is the Pasture in which they keep
their Calves; but the Manner is far different from any Thing you ever saw; they
may perhaps have a Stock of four or five
hundred to a thousand Head of Cattle
belonging to a Cow-Pen, these run as they
please in the great Woods, where there are
no Inclosures to stop them. In the Month
of *March* the Cows begin to drop their
Calves, then the Cow-Pen Master, with all
his Men, rides out to see and drive up the
Cows with all their new fallen Calves;

they being weak cannot run away so as to
escape, therefore are easily drove up, and
the Bulls and other Cattle follow them;
then they put these Calves into the Pasture,
and every Morning and Evening suffer the
Cows to come and suckle them, which done
they let the Cows out into the great Woods
to shift for their Food as well as they can;
whilst the Calf is sucking one Tit of the
Cow, the Woman of the Cow-Pen is milking one of the other Tits, so that she steals
some Milk from the Cow, who thinks she
is giving it to the Calf; as soon as the Cow
begins to go dry, and the Calf grows
Strong, they mark them, if they are Males
they cut them, and let them go into the
Wood. Every Year in *September* and *Octo-*
ber they drive up the Market Steers, that
are fat and of a proper Age, and kill them;
they say they are fat in *October*, but I am
sure they are not so in *May, June* and *July*;
they reckon that out of 100 Head of Cattle
they can kill about 10 or 12 Steers, and
four or five Cows a Year; so they reckon
that a Cow-Pen for every 100 Head of
Cattle brings about 40£ Sterling per Year.
The Keepers live chiefly upon Milk, for out

of their vast Herds, they do condescend to
tame Cows enough to keep their Family in
Milk, Whey, Curds, Cheese and Butter;
they also have Flesh in Abundance such as
it is, for they eat the old Cows and lean
Calves that are like to die.   The Cow-Pen
Men are hardy People, are almost continually on Horseback, being obliged to know
the Haunts of their Cattle.

" You see, Sir, what a wild set of Creatures our *English* Men grow into, when
they lose Society, and it is surprising to
think how many Advantages they throw
away, which our industrious Country-Men
would be glad of: Out of many hundred
Cows they will not give themselves the
trouble of milking more than will maintain
their Family."

.   .   .   .   .   .

" Since my last, we are got out of the
Settlements and into the Woods. The
Scene is changed, but not for the better.
I thought we were then so bad that we
had the Consolation of being out of Danger
of being worse, but I found myself mis-
taken.   The mutinous Spirit of the Men
encreases, but we will get the better of

that; we will see which will be tired first, they of deserving Punishments, or we of inflicting them. I cannot but say the very Face of the Country is enough to strike a Damp in the most resolute Mind; the Fatigues and Wants we suffer, added, are enough to dispirit common Men; nor should I blame them for being low spirited, but they are mutinous, and this came from a higher Spring than the Hardships here, for they were tainted in *Ireland* by the factious Cry against the L— L— Ld G—, and the Primate; the wicked Spirit instilled there by Pamphlets and Conversation, got amongst the common Soldiers, who, tho' they are *Englishmen*, yet are not the less stubborn and mutinous for that. They have the Impudence to pretend to judge of and blame every Step, not only of the Officers, but of the Ministry. They, every now and then, in their Defence say they are free *Englishmen*, and Protestants, and are not obliged to obey Orders if they are not fed with Bread, and paid with Money; now there is often only Bills to pay them with, and no Bread but *Indian* Corn. In fine, in *Europe* they were better fed than taught;

BRADDOCK'S ROAD NEAR FROSTBURG, MARYLAND

now they must be better taught than fed.
Indeed the Officers are as ill off about Food
as they, the General himself, who under-
stands good eating as well as any Man,
cannot find wherewithal to make a tolerable
Dinner of, though he hath two good Cooks
who could make an excellent Ragout out of
a Pair of Boots, had they but Materials to
toss them up with; the Provision in the
Settlements was bad, but here we can get
nothing but *Indian* Corn, or mouldy Bisket;
the fresh Bread we must bake in Holes in
the Ground having no Ovens, so besides
the Mustiness of the Flour, it is half Sand
and Dirt. We are happy if we can get
some rusty salt Pork, or Beef, which hath
been carried without Pickle; for as we
cannot carry Barrels on Horses, we are
forced to take out the Meat and put it in
Packs on Horses Backs; sometimes we get
a few live Cattle from the Cow-Pens, but
they are so lean that they are Carion and
unwholesome. To this is added, the Heat
of the Country, which occasions such Faint-
ness, that the Men can hardly carry their
Arms; and sometimes when these Heats are
a little relaxed, there comes such Storms of

Rain, Thunder and Lightening, that all the
Elements seems on Fire; Numbers of Pine
Trees struck to Shivers, and such Effects
of Lightening, that if not seen one could
hardly believe; yet we have not as yet had
one Man killed by Lightening, but we have
had several died by the Bite of Snakes,
which are mortal, and abound prodigiously
in the Swamps, through which we are often
forced to march; there is another Inconve-
niency, which, tho it seems small, has been
as teasing to me as the greater, that is a
Kind of Tick, or Forest Bug, that gets into
the Legs, and occasions Inflammations and
Ulcers, so that the wound itches and makes
one ready to tear off the Flesh; this hath
greatly distressed both Men and Officers,
and there is no Help nor Cure for it but
Patience: Indeed they seldom occasion
Lameness, tho' sometimes they do; a Sol-
dier of our Company was forced to have
his Leg cut off, for the Inflammation caused
by the many Bites mortifying. We have
nothing round us but Trees, Swamps, and
Thickets. I cannot conceive how we must
do if we are attacked, nor how we can get
up to attack; but the best is what the Gen-

eral said, to reassure the old Soldiers who
are all uneasy for Fear of being attack'd
on the long March in Defiles, his Excel-
lency with great Judiciousness says, that
where the Woods are too thick so as to
hinder our coming at them, they will hinder their coming at us.

" Just as I write this we hear the best
News I ever heard in my Life, the General
hath declared to the *Virginians*, that if they
do not furnish us with Waggons and Provisions in two Days, he will march back;
he has justly upbraided them for exposing
the King's Troops, by their Bragging and
false Promises.   They undertook to furnish
us with Horses, Bread and Beef, and really
have given nothing but Carion for Meat,
Indian Corn for Bread, Jades for Horses
which cannot carry themselves.   These
Assurances of furnishing every Thing has
deceived the General hitherto, and he, out
of Zeal for the Service, hath undergone the
utmost Difficulties; but now it is impossible to go farther without they comply with
the Promises, they were weak, or wicked
enough to make, for certainly they were
never able to perform them; it is surprizing

how they bragged before we left the Settlements, of what Plenty they would furnish us with at the Cow-Pens, and in the Woods; these Assurances has brought the General into the present Difficulties, and he has very justly told them, that if he marched any farther without a Supply, he should be justly charged with destroying his Majesty's Troops in the Deserts, and thereby occasion the Destruction of *Virginia* by encouraging the French; that if he was not supplied in two Days, he would march back, and lay their Breach of Faith before his Majesty.

" I now begin to hope that I shall once more have the Pleasure of seeing you, and the rest of my Friends. Pray acquaint my dear Mr. M —, that I desire he would not sell my Farm at —, since I hope soon to be over." [The rest relates to private affairs].

   .   .   .   .   .   .

" As the Intention of marching back continues, another Courier is to be sent, which Opportunity I take, not only to let you know I am well, but to desire my Cousin — would not send any Money to

Mr. — to be remitted to me in *Virginia*. As the Pen is in my Hand, I will give you an Account of a Diversion we had some Nights ago, it was an *Indian* Dancing, which I cannot call a Ball, though it was a Kind of Masquerade, the Habits being very antick; but this as every Thing in this Country is, was in the Stile of the Horrible; the Sal de Ball was covered with the Canopy of Heaven, and adorned with the twinkling Stars, a large Space of Grass was mark'd out for the Dancing-Place, round which we the Spectators stood, as at a Cricket-match in *England*, in the Centre of it was two Fires, at a small Distance from each other, which were designed as an Illumination to make the Dancers visible; near the Fires was seated the Musick, which were a number of Men and Women, with a Kind of Timbrels or small Kettle-Drums, made of real brass Kettles, covered with Deer Skins made like Parchment by the *Indians*, and these they beat, and keep good Time, although their Tunes are terrible and savage; they also sing much in the same Stile, creating Terror, Fear, and all dreadful Passions, but no pleasing ones.

After this Noise had gone on for some
Time, at ,once we heard a most dreadful
Shout, and a Band of horrid Figures rushed
into the Ring, with a Nimbleness hardly
conceivable; they struck the Ground in
exact Measure, answering the rough Musick; at once all the Descriptions of the
Fawns and Satyrs of the *Latin* Poets came
into my Mind, and indeed the *Indians*
seemed to be the same Kind of brown
dancing People, as lived under King *Fau-
nus*, some 3000 Years ago in *Italy*; they are
most chearful and loving to their Friends,
but implacable and cruel to their Enemies.
They drink and act when drunk much like
Silenus and his Satyrs; their whole Life is
spent in Hunting, War, and Dancing, what
they now perform'd was a War Dance; as
soon as this Surprize ceased the Dancers
followed one another, treading a large
Ring, round the two Fires and Music, and
ceased Singing; the Timbrels and Voices
in the Centre set up a Tune to which they
continued dancing, and follow'd one another
in the Ring with a very true Measure,
antick Postures, and high Bounds, that
would puzzle our best Harlequins to

imitate; soon after, to every five Dancers came out a Boy, carrying in their Hands flaming Splinters of light Wood instead of Torches, which cast a glim Light that made Things as distinguishable as at Noon-Day; and indeed the Surprisingness and Newness of the Spectacle made it not unpleasing; the Indians being dress'd, some in Furrs, some with their Hair ornamented with Feathers, others with the Heads of Beasts; their Bodies naked, appearing in many Places, painted with various Colours, and their Skins so rubbed with Oyl as to glitter against the Light; their Waists were girded round with Bear or Deer Skins with the Hair on, and artificial Tails fixed to many of them that hung down near unto the Ground. After they had danced some Time in a Ring, the Music ceased, the Dancers divided into two Parties, and set up the most horrid Song or Cry, that ever I heard, the Sound would strike Terror into the stoutest Heart. They then formed themselves into two Bodies, four deep, all which they did, still dancing to the Tune and Measure; they ceased singing, and the Music began, on which the two Bodies run

in at each other, acting all the Parts the
Indians use in their Manner of Fight, avoiding Shot, and striving to surround their
Enemies. Some Time past in this Manner,
and then at the Signal of a dismal Cry the
Dancers all at once rushed out again, leaving one only behind them, who was supposed to have mastered his Enemy; he
struck the Ground with his Tomohawk or
Club, as if he was killing one lying there,
then acting the Motions of scalping, and
then holding up a real dried Scalp, which
before hung upon him amongst his Orna-
ments; he then sung out the great Achive-
ments which some of their Nation had
performed against the *French*, told the
Names of the *Indian* Warriors, and how
many of *French* each had scalped, and then
the Dance ended, *&c.*"

. . . . .

" In my last I acquainted you with the
joyful News that our General resolved not
to be any longer deceived by the *Virginians*,
Orders were given for our March back, but
the Day before that was appointed there
arrived five Quakers decently dressed, they
were pure plump Men, on brave fat Horses,

which, by the way, were the first plump
Creatures I had seen in this Country.
Then, as I told you before, I believed *Virginia* was peopled by *Pharaoh's* lean Kine,
but these Quakers seem to come from the
Land of *Goshen*, they looked like Christian
People; they went directly to his Excel-
lence, and Curiosity carried us all to the
general Quarters. They came with Thanks
to the General from the People of Pensilvania, for the great Labour he had gone
through in advancing so far into the Wilderness for the Protection of his Majesty's
dutiful Subjects. They acquainted him
further, that they had been cutting Roads
to meet him with a Number of Waggons
loaded with Flour, Cheese, Bacon, and
other Provision; though this was good
News I did not half like it, I fear'd it
would occasion our Stay, and prevent our
marching back; besides it was ominous,
your Cheese and your Bacon being the
Baits that draw Rats to Destruction, and it
proved but too true; this Bait drew us into
a Trap where happy was he that came off
with the Loss of his Tail only. This
Evening we saw the Road and Waggons,

and the Men eat, this was a Duty so long
disused, that it was a Tour of Fatigue to
the Teeth. The Fellows who drove the
Waggons, tho' they would have made but
a shabby Figure amongst our *Hampshire*
Carters, yet here they looked like Angels,
compared with the long, lank, yellow-faced
Virginians, who at best are a half-starved,
ragged, dirty Set; if by Accident they can
clear enough by their Tobacco to buy a
Coat, they rather chuse a half-wore gaudy
Rag, than a substantial coarse Cloth, or
Kersey; they are the very Opposites to the
Pensilvanians, who buy Coats of Cloth so
strong as to last as long as the Garments of
the *Israelites* in their March through the
Desert; a Coat serves a Man for his Life
and yet looks fresh, but this comes from
their never wearing them at Home; when
out of Sight they work half naked. They
are a very frugal People, and if they were
not so would be as beggarly as their Neigh-
bours the *Virginians*. The Ground does
not bear half the Crops as in *England*; they
have no Market but by Sea, and that very
dull, if you consider they are forced to put
their Flour in Barrels after grinding and

sifting, all at their own Charge, and no
Consideration thereof in the Price; whilst
the *English* Farmer only threshes his
Wheat, and sends it to Market. Tho' *Pensilvania* is a Paradise to *Virginia*, it is a very
poor Country compared to *England*, and no
Man in his Senses can live with Comfort in
England stays here; as soon as they get
Estates they come over to *England*. The
Proprietor, a most worthy Gentleman, and
universally admired, went over, and out of
Complaisance staid a little Time with
them, but soon returned back to *England*,
where he resides. If *Pennsylvania* could be
agreeable to any one, it would be so to
him, who is one of the most amiable Men
living, and the whole People used their
utmost Endeavors to make the Place agreeable; but alas, the Intemperature of the
Climate, the Nearness and Frugality in
their Manner of Living, necessary to carry
on the Cultivation; the Labor that most
are forced to undergo to live, prevent their
giving Way to Pleasure, and the rest, as
soon as they by Labor and Frugality get
enough to come to *England*, leave that
Country, so there are not People enough at

Ease to make an agreeable Society; nor to occasion those Improvements in Gardens, Buildings, and Parks, as would make Life agreeable, much less is their Numbers enough of Rich to afford encouragement to support public Diversions; so that *America* is a very disagreeable Place, the least Shire-Town in *England* has more Pleasures than the best Town in *North America*.

" But to return to our Quakers, the Chief of them told the General that he feared greatly for the Safety of the Army; that the Woods, the farther we went, would be the more dangerous, and the *French* were a subtle and daring Enemy, and would not neglect any Opportunity of surprising us; that the further we went the more difficult it would be to supply us with Provisions, and that the Country was not worth keeping, much less conquering. The *French* not yet knowing our Force were in Terror, and if he sent would perhaps come into a Treaty; that Peace was a heavenly Thing; and as for the Country in Dispute it was misrepresented by those Projectors, who had some private Advantage; for it was fit for none but *Indians*, the Soil bad, far from the Sea, and Navigation; therefore he thought if the *French* would abandon and destroy their Forts, and we do the same, and leave the Lands to their rightful Owners the *Indians*, on Condition that that Nation should pay some Furrs and Deer Skins, by Way of Tribute, to our most gracious King *George*, a Pacification might be established till the Matter was made up before his Majesty. That General *Oglethorp* had in that Manner settled all Differences with the *Spaniards* on the Southern Frontiers, towards *Florida*, and the Accord lasted to this Day; on the other Hand, he said, that if the *French* refused, then the *Indians*, who are a free and warlike Nation, and much too powerful to be despised, would probably take our Side; if we would pull down the *French* Forts, and our own also, they would be the guard of our Colonies with very small Expense to *England*.

" The General not only heard this Proposal with Pleasure, and communicated it to most of the Officers, but doubted if he had Power to execute it. Some of the Braggadocio *Virginians*, who last Year ran away so stoutly, began to clamor against

the Quakers and the General; so we
marched on; the General got as far as the
Meadows, where, to hasten our March, he
fortified and intrenched a Camp, and left
the heavy Baggage, sick Men, and spare
Provision &c, and to cover our Communication, he left Colonel *Dunbar* with 800
Men. This place was the only one where
regular Troops could make Use of their
Discipline and Arms, and it is all open
Ground, therefore the General made this
Camp as a Place of Arms, where a Forti-
fication being erected would supply the
Army as they should want, and might
receive, and lay up the Provisions in
Safety, as they arrived from *Pennsylvania*;
the General also said, that as this Place
was on the West Side of the *Allegane*
Mountains, it preserved his Majesty's
Rights against the *French*, who pretended
that those Mountains bounded his Majesty's
Dominions. Here we halted and refreshed
ourselves bravely, by the Help of the
Pensilvania Provisions, and of Deer, wild
Turkeys, and Game of several other Kinds
brought in by the *Indians*, which though
we should deem it bad enough in *England*,

for there is not above one Deer in ten that
is fat, yet here our former Wants made
these delicious.

"On the 4th of *July* our *Indians* were
defeated in the Woods by the *French* Parties; a few only was killed, but their chief
Man was taken; the *French* have treated
them very kindly, and declare they intend
no War against the *Indians*. The General
is apprehensive this will make an ill Impression on them, therefore does not care to
trust them any further; he has publickly
said he will advance himself with 1200
Men, drive the Enemy out of the Woods,
and invest *Fort Du Quesne*; he is resolved
to be prepared for all Accidents, therefore
leaves Colonel *Dunbar* with a strong Party
to make good this Camp. The Ground
round the Camp is open, and the Situation
so advantageous, that this Camp is defens-
ible against all the Efforts the *French* can
make, if any Accident, should happen to
the General; and he has declared, he has
put it in this Condition, that his Majesty's
Affairs may not suffer if he should miscarry.

"The General seems very anxious about
marching through the Woods, and gave

very particular Orders; Powder and Bullet were given out, and every Thing fit for Action; two Lieutenant-Colonels were ordered to command the advanced Party. The General followed with the Gross of the two Regiments from *Europe*, the *Americans* followed, and the Rear was brought up by Captain *Dumary's*, and another Independent Company. We marched on in this Manner without being disturbed, and thought we had got over our greatest Difficulties, for we look'd upon our March through the Woods to be such: We were sure we should be much above a Match for the *French*, if once we got into the open Ground near the Forts, where we could use our Arms. We had a Train, and a gallant Party of Sailors for working our Guns, full sufficient to master better works than those of the *French* Forts, according to the Intelligence we had of them. Then we march'd on, and when within about ten Miles of Fort *Du Quesne*, we were, on a sudden, charged by Shot from the Woods. Every Man was alert, did all we could, but the Men dropped like Leaves in *Autumn*, all was Confusion, and in Spight of what the Officers and bravest Men could do, Numbers run away, nay fired on us, that would have forced them to rally. I was wounded in one Leg, and in the other Heel, so could not go, but sat down at the Foot of a Tree, praying of every one that run by, that they would help me off; an *American Virginian* turned to me, Yes, Countryman, says he, I will put you out of your Misery, these Dogs shall not burn you; he then levelled his Piece at my Head, I cried out and dodged him behind the Tree, the Piece went off and missed me, and he run on; soon after Lieutenant *Grey*, with a Party of *Dumary's* Company came by, who brought up the Rear; the Firing was now Quite ceased, he told me the General was wounded, and got me carried off. When we arrived at the *Meadows*, we found Colonel *Dunbar* did not think it expedient to wait for the *French* there, but retired, and carried us, the wounded, with him to *Will's Creek*. I have writ till I am faint."

CHAPTER VII

SPARKS AND ATKINSON ON BRADDOCK'S ROUTE [46]

SEVERAL months ago we received from that indefatigable delver in the early annals of our country, Jared Sparks, Esq., of Salem, Massachusetts, a letter containing some valuable information as to the route of General Braddock after leaving Gist's farm, not far from where Connelsville now stands. That letter we, for reasons which it is unnecessary to mention, have withheld from publication; but those reasons no longer existing, we now publish it — premising only a few introductory remarks.

Mr. Sparks, as the biographer of Washington and as the collator of his papers, and as a most indefatigable searcher after the whole truth in our early history, en-

[46] This chapter is from Neville B. Craig's *The Olden Time*, vol. ii., pp. 465–468, 539–544.

joyed extraordinary advantages, so that his statements in all such matters should always command the utmost confidence. There is in the possession of the Pennsylvania Historical Society a draught of " the Monongahela and Youghiogany rivers" taken by Joseph Shippen, Jr., in 1759.[47] On this draught the route of General Braddock is distinctly laid down from Cumberland to Stewart's Crossings, now Connelsville, and thence to a point about twelve or fourten miles, nearly due north, and of course some four or five miles east of the Youghiogany. From that point the line of march is not laid down until within about six miles of the Monongahela river, at Braddock's first ford, about one mile and a half below McKeesport; from that point it is distinctly traced across the Monongahela twice to the field of battle. As Mr. Shippen was Brigade Major in General Forbes' army, and in that capacity visited this place within four years after Braddock's defeat, we may well suppose that he had accurate information as to the route of that unfortunate General.

[47] See *Historic Highways of America*, vol. v.

Extract of a letter from Jared Sparks, Esq., to the editor of the *Olden Time*.

"Salem, Mass., Feb. 18th, 1847.

"Dear Sir:— There is a copy of the 'Memorial' which you mentioned in the Library of Harvard College which I believe is complete. I shall obtain it soon, and will have the missing pages copied and forward to you the manuscript. I suppose you wish it sent by mail. I once compared this translation with the original[48] and found it clumsily executed, but the substance is probably retained.

" Having heretofore examined with care the details of Braddock's expedition, I am persuaded that the following, as far as it goes, is a correct account of his march from Gist's plantation:

" On the 30th of June the army forded the Youghiogany at Stewart's Crossings and then passed a rough road over a mountain. A few days onward they came to a great swamp which detained them part of a day in clearing a road. They next advanced to Salt Lick Creek, now called Jacob's Creek, where a council of war was

[48] Preserved in the library of Harvard University.

held on the 3d of July to consider a suggestion of Sir John St. Clair that Colonel
Dunbar's detachment should be ordered to
join the main body. This proposal was
rejected on the ground that Dunbar could
not join them in less than thirteen days;
that this would cause such a consumption
of provisions as to render it necessary to
bring forward another convoy from Fort
Cumberland; and that in the meantime the
French might be strengthened by a rein-
forcement, which was daily expected at Fort
Duquesne — and moreover; the two divi-
sions could not move together after their
junction.

"On the 4th the army again marched
and advanced to Turtle Creek, about twelve
miles from its mouth, where they arrived
on the 7th inst. I suppose this to have
been the eastern branch or what is now
called Rush Creek, and that the place at
which they encamped was a short distance
northerly from the present village of
Stewartsville. It was General Braddock's
intention to cross Turtle Creek, and approach Fort Duquesne on the other side;
but the banks were so precipitous, and

presented such obstacles to crossing with his artillery and heavy baggage that he hesitated, and Sir John St. Clair went out with a party to reconnoitre. On his return, before night, he reported that he had found the ridge which led to Fort Duquesne but that considerable work would be necessary to prepare a road for crossing Turtle Creek. This route was finally abandoned, and on the 8th the army marched eight miles and encamped not far from the Monongahela, west of the Youghiogany and near what is called in an old map 'Sugar Run.' When Braddock reached this place it was his design to pass through the narrows, but he was informed by the guides who had been out to explore that the passage was very difficult, about two miles in length, with a river on the left and a high mountain on the right, and that much work must be done to make it passable for carriages. At the same time he was told that there were two good fords across the Monongahela where the water was shallow and the banks not steep. With these views of the case he determined to cross the fords the next morning. The order of march was given

out and all the arrangements were made
for an early movement.

"About eight o'clock on the morning of
the 9th the advanced division under Colonel Gage crossed the ford and pushed
forward. After the whole army had
crossed and marched about a mile, Braddock received a note from Colonel Gage,
giving notice that he had passed the second
ford without difficulty. A little before two
o'clock the whole army had crossed this
ford and was arranged in the order of
march on the plain near Frazer's house.
Gage with the advanced party was then
ordered to march, and while the main body
was yet standing on the plain the action
began near the river. Not a single man
of the enemy had before been seen.

"The distance by the line of march from
Stewart's Crossing to Turtle Creek, or
Brush Creek, was about thirty miles. At
this point the route was changed almost to
a right angle in marching to the Monongahela. The encampment was probably two
or three miles from the bank of the river,
for Colonel Gage marched at the break of
day and did not cross the ford till eight

o'clock.   During the whole march from the
Great Meadows the pickets and sentinels
were frequently assailed by scouting parties of French and Indians and several men
were killed.   Mr. Gist acted as the General's guide.   On the 4th of July two Indians
went out to reconnoitre the country toward
Fort Duquesne; and Mr. Gist also on the
same day, in a different direction.   They
were gone two days, and all came in sight
of the fort, but brought back no important
intelligence.   The Indians contrived to kill
and scalp a French officer whom they found
shooting within half a mile of the fort.

"The army seldom marched more than
six miles a day and commonly not so much.
From Stewart's Crossing to Turtle Creek
there were six encampments.   During one
day the army halted.

"I shall be much pleased to see Mr.
Atkinson's map.   His knowledge of the
ground will enable him to delineate Braddock's route much more accurately than it
can be done from any sources now available.

I am, Sir, respectfully yours,

Jared Sparks.

Neville B. Craig, Esq., Pittsburgh."

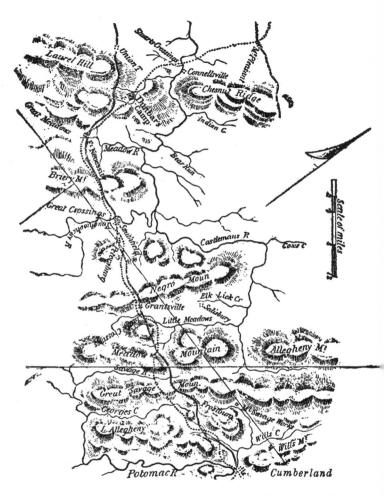

MIDDLETON'S MAP OF BRADDOCK'S ROAD (1847)

[*Braddock's Road is shown as dotted line. The double line is the present
route from Cumberland to Ft. Necessity*]

Since the foregoing letter was in type we
have received from Mr. T. C. Atkinson of
Cumberland, Maryland, lately employed on
the Pittsburgh and Connelsville Rail Road,
a very able and interesting article on the
subject of Braddock's route to the Monongahela, with a very beautiful map of the
country, by Mr. Middleton, one of Mr.
Atkinson's assistants on the survey for the
railroad.   The article of Mr. Atkinson, and
the map, furnish all the information as to
the march of General Braddock's army
which can now be hoped for.

Mr. Atkinson had for years devoted much
time to the examination of the route of the
army of Braddock eastward, and some
distance westward of Cumberland, and his
late employ along the Youghiogany and
Monongahela afforded him an opportunity
to complete his work.

As a striking evidence of the accuracy of
his researches, we will mention that in
tracing the route he was much surprised
and puzzled by what seemed the strange
divergence of the army from the Youghiogany river after passing it at Stewart's
Crossings.   Yet the traditionary evidence

and marks on the ground seemed to establish beyond doubt the fact that the army had passed far into the interior of our present county of Westmoreland, and near to Mount Pleasant, crossing the line of the Pittsburgh and Greensburg Turnpike road. This seemed so far from the natural and direct route that even the strong traditionary and other evidence, could not entirely remove the possibility of doubt.   Mr. Atkinson himself was entirely satisfied as to the correctness of his own conclusions, but of course would be gratified to receive a confirmation, in an authentic shape, of his own convictions.

Just at that crisis we received the letter from Mr. Sparks, which precedes these remarks, thus settling most conclusively the verity of many of the traditions current in the country as to the erratic course of Braddock's army from Stewart's Crossings to the Monongahela river.

We are, deeply indeed, indebted to Mr. Atkinson, and also to his assistant, Mr. Middleton, for their very valuable contribution in illustration of the early history of this country.

The Pittsburgh and Connelsville Rail Road project cannot be regarded as an entirely fruitless effort; it has, at least, produced this most valuable historical essay.

. All additional information in relation to those early scenes must possess interest to every intelligent American; and we rejoice in the opportunity of placing Mr. Atkinson's valuable communication and the accompanying map before the readers of the *Olden Time :*

'' The interest with which the routes of celebrated expeditions are regarded, and the confusion which attends them after the lapse of years, is well exemplified in the case of Hannibal, whose march toward Rome, in order to divert their army from the siege of Capua, was totally lost in the course of a few centuries. The constant blunders of Livy in copying first from one writer, and then from another who made him take a different path, justify a recent English historian who went to Italy to see the ground for himself, in saying that the Punic War was almost as hard in the writing as the fighting.

" As the time is coming when the road by which the unfortunate Braddock marched to his disastrous field will be invested with antiquarian interest akin to that attending Hannibal's route, or rather the *via scelerata*, by which the Fabian family marched out of Rome, I have thought it time not idly spent to attempt to pursue its scattered traces as far as it is in my power, among more pressing occupations. In this sketch I do not design to pursue it to its extent, but only to identify it in those parts where it has been convenient for me to visit it and in others to shadow out its general direction. Where it is obscure I hope to have opportunities to examine it at a future day.

" Of the well conducted expedition of Colonel Bouquet and its precise path, the publications of Mr. Hutchins, the geographer, who was one of the engineers, leaves us very well informed. It is presumable that similar details would be found of the march of 1755 if it had had a successful termination. The three engineers who were in the field were wounded; and it is probable their papers fell into the hands of the enemy or were lost in the flight.

" General Braddock landed at Alexandria on the 20th of February, 1755. The selection of this port for the debarcation of the troops, was censured at the time, though it is probable it had the approval of Washington. The two regiments he brought with him were very defective in numbers, having but about five hundred men each, and it was expected their ranks would be recruited in America. It is shown by the repeated requests on this point made by the General at Cumberland that this expectation was vain. After numerous delays, and a conference with the Royal Governors, we find General Braddock *en route* on the 24th of April when he had reached Fredricktown in Maryland. Passing thence through Winchester, Va., he reached Fort Cumberland about the 9th of May. Sir John Sinclair, Deputy Quarter Master General, had preceded him to this point about two weeks.[49]

[49] " Many misstatements are prevalent in the country adjacent to the line of march, especially east of Cumberland, the traditionary name of Braddock's route being often applied to routes we know he did not pur-

"The army struck the Little Cacapehon
(though pronounced Cacapon, I have used
for the occasion the spelling of Washington
and various old documents), about six miles
above its mouth, and following the stream
encamped on the Virginia side of the
Potomac preparatory to crossing into Maryland. The water is supposed to have been
high at the time, as the spot is known as
the Ferry-fields, from the army having
been ferried over. This was about the 4th
or 5th of May.

"The army thence pursued the banks of
the river, with a slight deviation of route
at the mouth of the South Branch, to the
village of Old Town, known at that time
sue. It is probable the ground of the application consists in their having been used by the Quarter Master's
men in bringing on those Pennsylvania wagons and pack
horses procured by Dr. Franklin, with so much trouble
and at so great expense of truth. Sir John Sinclair wore
a Hussar's cap, and Franklin made use of the circum-
stance to terrify the German settlers with the belief that
he was a Hussar who would administer to them the
tyrannical treatment they had experienced in their own
country if they did not comply with his wishes. It is
singular that a small brook and an obscure country road
in Berkley County, Virginia, bear the name of Sir John's
Run, and Sir John's Road, supposed to be taken from
the name of this officer.

as the Shawnee Old Town, modern use having dropped the most characteristic part of the name. This place, distant about eight miles from the Ferry-fields, was known at that early day as the residence of Col. Thomas Cresap, an English settler, and the father of the hero of Logan's speech. The road proceeded thence parallel with the river and at the foot of the hills, till it passes the narrows of Will's Mountain, when it struck out a shorter line coincident with the present county road, and lying between the railroad and the mountain, to Fort Cumberland.

" From the Little Cacapehon to this point the ground was comparatively easy, and the road had been generally judiciously chosen. Thenceforward the character of the ground was altered, not so much in the general aspect of the country as that the march was about to abandon the valleys, and now the real difficulties of the expedition may be said to commence.

" The fort had been commenced the previous year, after the surrender at the Great Meadows, by Col. Innes, who had with him the two independent companies of New York and South Carolina. It mounted ten four pounders, besides swivels, and was favorably situated to keep the hostile Indians in check.[50]

"The army now consisted of 1000 regulars, 30 sailors, and 1200 provincials, besides a train of artillery. The provincials were from New York and Virginia; one company from the former colony was commanded by Captain Gates, afterwards the hero of Saratoga. On the 8th of June, Braddock having, through the interest and exertions of Dr. Franklin, principally, got 150 wagons and 2000 horses from Pennsylvania, was ready to march.

"*Scaroodaya*, successor to the Half-King of the Senecas, and *Monacatootha*, whose acquaintance Washington has made on the Ohio, on his mission to Le Bœuf, with about 150 Indians, Senecas, and Delawares, accompanied him.   .   .   .

"The first brigade under Sir Peter

[50] "The original name of Cumberland was Cucucbetuc, and from its favorable position on the Potomac, was most probably the site of a Shawnee village, like Old Town; moreover, it was marked by an Indian name, a rare occurrence in this vicinity, if any judgment may be drawn from the few that have been preserved.

Halket, led the way on the 8th, and on the 9th the main body followed. Some idea of the difficulties they encountered, may be had when we perceive they spent the third night only five miles from the first. The place of encampment which is about one third of a mile from the toll-gate on the National Road, is marked by a copious spring bearing Braddock's name.

"For reasons not easy to divine, the route across Will's Mountain first adopted for the national road was selected instead of the more favorable one through the narrows of Will's Creek, to which the road has been changed within a few years for the purpose of avoiding that formidable ascent. The traces are very distinct on the east and west slopes, the modern road crossing it frequently. From the western foot, the route continued up Braddock's Run to the forks of the stream, where Clary's tavern now stands, nine miles from Cumberland, when it turned to the left, in order to reach a point on the ridge favorable to an easy descent into the valley of George's Creek. It is surprising that having reached this high ground, the

favorable spur by which the National Road
accomplishes the ascent of the Great Savage Mountain, did not strike the attention
of the engineers, as the labor requisite to
surmount the barrier from the deep valley
of George's Creek, must have contributed
greatly to those bitter complaints which
Braddock made against the Colonial Governments for their failure to assist him
more effectively in the transportation
department.

" Passing then a mile to the south of
Frostburg, the road approaches the east
foot of Savage Mountain, which it crosses
about one mile south of the National Road,
and thence by very favorable ground
through the dense forests of white pine
peculiar to this region, it got to the north
of the National Road, near the gloomy
tract called the *Shades of Death*. This was
the 15th of June, when the dense gloom of
the summer woods and the favorable shelter
which those enormous pines would give an
Indian enemy, must have made a most
sensible impression on all minds, of the
insecurity of their mode of advance.

" This doubtless had a share in causing

the council of war held at the Little
Meadows[51] the next day. To this place,
distant only about twenty miles from Cumberland, Sir John Sinclair and Major Chapman had been dispatched on the 27th of
May, to build a fort; the army having been
seven days in reaching it, it follows as the
line of march was upwards of three miles
long, the rear was just getting under way
when the advance were lighting their
evening fires.

[51] " This interesting locality lies at the west foot of
the Meadow Mountain, which is one of the most important of the Alleghany Ridges, in Pennsylvania especially, where it constitutes the dividing ridge between
the eastern and western waters. A rude entrenchment,
about half a mile north of the Inn on the National Road,
kept by Mr. Huddleson, marks the site of this fort.
This is most probably the field of a skirmish spoken of
in frontier history, between a Mr. Parris, with a scouting party from Fort Cumberland, and the Sieur Donville, commanding some French and Indians, in which
the French officer was slain. The tradition is distinctly
preserved in the vicinity, with a misapprehension of
Washington's participation in it, arising probably from
the partial resemblance between the names of Donville
and Jumonville. From the positiveness of the information, in regard to the battle ground, conflicting with
what we know of Jumonville's death, it seems probable
enough that this was the scene of this Indian skirmish;
and as such, it possesses a classic interest, valuable in
proportion to the scarcity of such places.

" Here it may be well enough to clear up an obscurity which enters into many narratives of these early events, from confusing the names of the *Little Meadows* and *Great Meadows*, *Little Crossings* and *Great Crossings*, which are all distinct localities.

" The *Little Meadows* have been described as at the foot of Meadow Moutain; it is well to note that the *Great Meadows* are about thirty-one miles further west, and near the east foot of Laurel Hill.

" By the *Little Crossings* is meant the Ford of Casselman's River, a tributary of the Youghiogheny; and by the *Great Crossings*, the passage of the Youghiogheny itself. The Little Crossing is two miles west of the Little Meadows, and the Great Crossing seventeen miles further west.

" The conclusion of the council was to push on with a picked force of 1200 men and 12 pieces of cannon; and the line of march, now more compact was resumed on the 19th. Passing over ground to the south of the Little Crossings, and of the village of Grantsville, which it skirted, the army spent the night of the 21st at the Bear Camp, a locality I have not been able

to identify, but suppose it to be about mid-
way to the Great Crossings, which it
reached on the 23d.   The route thence to
the Great Meadows or Fort Necessity was
well chosen, though over a mountainous
tract, conforming very nearly to the ground
now occupied by the National Road, and
keeping on the dividing ridge between the
waters flowing into the Youghiogheny on
the one hand and the Cheat River on the
other.   Having crossed the Youghiogheny,
we are now on the classic ground of Washington's early career, where the skirmish
with Jumonville, and Fort Necessity, indi-
cate the country laid open for them in the
previous year.   About one mile west of the
Great Meadows and near the spot now
marked as Braddock's Grave, the road
struck off more to the north-west, in order to
reach a pass through Laurel Hill that would
enable them to strike the Youghiogheny,
at a point afterwards known as Stewart's
Crossing and about half a mile below the
present town of Connellsville.   This part
of the route is marked by the farm known
as Mount Braddock.   This second crossing
of the Youghiogheny was effected on the

30th of June.   The high grounds interven-
ing between the river and its next tributary,
Jacob's Creek, though trivial in comparison
with what they had already passed, it may
be supposed, presented serious obstacles to
the troops, worn out with previous exertions.   On the 3d of July a council of war
was held at Jacob's Creek, to consider the
propriety of bringing forward Col. Dunbar with the reserve, and although urged
by Sir John Sinclair with, as one may suppose, his characteristic vehemence, the
measure was rejected on sufficient grounds.
From the crossing of Jacob's Creek, which
was at the point where Welchhanse's Mill
now stands, about 1½ miles below Mount
Pleasant, the route stretched off to the
north, crossing the Mount Pleasant turnpike
near the village of the same name, and
thence by a more westerly course, passing
the Great Sewickley near Painter's Salt
Works, thence south and west of the Post
Office of Madison and Jacksonville, it
reached the Brush Fork of Turtle Creek.
It must strike those who examine the map
that the route, for some distance, in the rear
and ahead of Mount Pleasant, is out of the

proper direction for Fort Duquesne, and accordingly we find on the 7th of July, Gen. Braddock in doubt as to his proper way of proceeding. The crossing of Brush Creek, which he had now reached, appeared to be attended with so much hazard that parties were sent to reconnoitre, some of whom advanced so far as to kill a French officer within half a mile of Fort Duquesne.

" Their examinations induced a great divergence to the left, and availing himself of the valley of Long Run, which he turned into, as is supposed, at Stewartsville, passing by the place now known as Samson's Mill, the army made one of the best marches of the campaign and halted for the night at a favorable depression between that stream and Crooked Run and about two miles from the Monongahela. At this spot, about four miles from the battle ground, which is yet well known as Braddock's Spring, he was rejoined by Washington on the morning of the 9th of July.

" The approach to the river was now down the valley of Crooked Run to its mouth, where the point of fording is still manifest, from a deep notch in the west bank, though rendered somewhat obscure by the improved navigation of the river. The advance, under Col. Gage, crossed about 8 o'clock, and continued by the foot of the hill bordering the broad river bottom to the second fording, which he had effected nearly as soon as the rear had got through the first.

" The second and last fording at the mouth of Turtle Creek was in full view of the enemy's position, and about one mile distant. By 1 o'clock the whole army had gained the right bank, and was drawn up on the bottom land, near Frazier's house (spoken of by Washington as his stopping place on his mission to Le Bœuf), and about ¾ of a mile distant from the ambuscade."

CHAPTER VIII

BRADDOCK'S ROAD IN HISTORY

THE narrow swath of a road cut through the darkling Alleghenies by General Braddock has been worth all it cost in time and treasure. Throughout the latter half of the eighteenth century it was one of the main thoroughfares into the Ohio valley, and when, at the dawning of the nineteenth, the United States built our first and greatest public highway, the general alignment of Braddock's Road between Cumberland and the last range of the Alleghenies — Laurel Hill — was the course pursued. In certain localities this famed national boulevard, the Cumberland Road, was built upon the very bed of Braddock's road, as Braddock's road had been built partly upon the early Washington's Road which followed the path of Indian, buffalo, and mound-building aborigines. Nowhere in America can the evolution of road-building be studied to such advantage as between Cumberland, Maryland and Uniontown, Pennsylvania.

For some years after Braddock's defeat his route to and fro between the Monongahela and Potomac was used only by scouting parties of whites and marauding Indians, and many were the swift encounters that took place upon its overgrown narrow track. In 1758 General Forbes built a new road westward from Carlisle, Pennsylvania rather than follow Braddock's ill-starred track, for reasons described in another volume of the present series.[52] Forbes frightened the French forever from the " Forks of the Ohio " and erected Fort Pitt on the ruins of the old Fort Duquesne. In 1763 Colonel Bouquet led a second army across the Alleghenies, on Forbes's Road, relieved Fort Pitt and put an end to Pontiac's Rebellion. By the time of Forbes's expedition Braddock's Road was somewhat filled with undergrowth, and was not cut at all through the last and most important eight miles of the course to Fort Duquesne. Forbes had some plans of using this route,

[52] *Historic Highways of America*, vol. v., ch. 4.

" if only as a blind," but finally his whole force proceeded over a new road. However, certain portions of Braddock's Road had been cleared early in the campaign when Forbes thought it would be as well to have " two Strings to one Bow." It was not in bad condition.[53]

This new northern route, through Lancaster, Carlisle, Bedford (Reastown), and Ligonier, Pennsylvania, became as important, if not more so, than Braddock's course from Cumberland to Braddock, Pennsylvania. As the years passed Braddock's Road seems to have regained something of its early prestige, and throughout the Revolutionary period it was perhaps of equal consequence with any route toward the Ohio, especially because of Virginia's interest in and jealousy of the territory about Pittsburg. When, shortly after the close of the Revolution, the great flood of immigration swept westward, the current was divided into three streams near the Potomac; one went southward over the Virgi-

---

[53] *Bouquet Papers, MSS.* Preserved in British Museum: Forbes to Pitt, July 10; Forbes to Bouquet, August 2; Bouquet au Forbes, July 26, 1758.

nian route through Cumberland Gap to Kentucky; the other two burst over Forbes's and Braddock's Roads. Some pictures of the latter are vividly presented in early records of pilgrims who chose its rough path to gain the El Dorado beyond the Appalachian mountain barriers.

William Brown, an emigrant to Kentucky from Hanover, Virginia, over Braddock's Road in 1790 has left a valuable itinerary of his journey, together with interesting notes, entitled *Observances and Occurrences*. The itinerary is as follows:

	MILES
To Hanover Court House, . .	16
To Edmund Taylor's, . .	16
To Parson Todd's, Louisa, .	20
To Widow Nelson's . . .	20
To Brock's Bridge, Orange Co., .	9
To Garnet's Mill	5
To Bost. Ord'y, near Hind's House.	7
To Raccoon Ford, on Rapidan or Porters, ...	6
To Culpepper Co.-House, .	10
To Pendleton's Ford, on Rappahannock, ...	10

To Douglass's Tavern, or Wick-
    liffe's House, ... 13

To Chester's Gap, Blue Ridge,   . 8

To Lehu Town, ... 3

To Ford of Shenandore River,
    Frederick, ... 2

To Stevensburg, ... 10

To Brown's Mill, ... 2

To Winchester, ... 6

To Gasper Rinker's, .   .   . 11

To Widow Lewis's, Hampshire,   . 11

To Crock's Tav., ... 9

To Reynold's, on the So. Branch
    Potowmack, ... 13

To Frankford Town, .   .   . 8

To Haldeman's Mills,   .   . 4

To North Branch, Potomack, .   . 3

To Gwyn's Tav., at the Fork of
    Braddock's old road, Alleghany
    Co., Maryland,   .   .   . 3

To Clark's Store, ... 6

To Little Shades of Death,   .   . 12

To Tumblestone Tav., or the Little
    Meadows, ... 3

To Big Shades of Death, .   .   . 2

To Mountain Tav., or White Oak
    Springs, ... 2

To Simpson's Tav., Fayette Co.,
    Pennsylvania, ... 6
To Big Crossing of Yoh, . . . 9
To Carrol's Tavern, ... 12
To Laurel Hill, ... 6
To Beason Town, ... 6
To Redstone, Old Fort, . . . 12
To Washington Town, Washington
    Co., Penn., ... 23
To Wheeling, Old Fort, Ohio Co.,
    Vir., ... 35
                         ‾‾‾
                    359 [54]

Mr. Brown's notes of the journey over the mountains are:

" Set out from Hanover Friday 6th August 1790 arrived at Redstone Old Fort about the 25th Inst. The road is pretty good until you get to the Widow Nelson's, then it begins to be hilly and continues generally so till you get to the Blue Ridge — pretty well watered. Racoon ford on Rapidan is rather bad. The little mountains are frequently in view After you pass Widow Nelson's. Pendleton's ford on Rappahanock is pretty good. In going over

[54] Speed's *The Wilderness Road*, pp. 56–57.

Chester gap you ride about 5 miles among
the mountains before you get clear, a good
many fine springs in the Mo. between the
Blue Ridge and the Alleghany Mo. appears
to be a fine country, altho the land is pretty
much broken. At Shenandore ford there
is two branches of the river to cross and it
is bad fording. But there is a ferry a little
below the ford. There is a very cool
stream of water about 14 miles below Winchester. This is a well watered country
but springs are rather scarce on the road,
at Winchester there are several fine
springs. The South branch of Potowmack
has a good ford, also the North branch.
Soon after you pass Gwyns Tavern in
Maryland you enter upon the Alleghany
Mo. and then you have a great deal of bad
road, many ridges of Mo. —the Winding
Ridge — Savage, Negro, etc. and Laurel
Hill which is the last, but before you get
to the Mount, there is some stony bad road
between the Widow Lewis' and the Mo.
after you pass Clark's store in the Mo. you
get into a valley of very pretty oak land.
In many places while you are in the Mo.
there is very good road between the ridges.

Just before you get to the Little Shades of Death there is a.tract of the tallest pines I ever saw. The Shades of Death are dreary looking valleys, growing up with tall cypress and other trees and has a dark gloomy appearance. Tumblestones, or the Little Meadows is a fine plantation with beautiful meadow ground. Crossing of Yoh, is a pretty good ford. There is some very bad road about here. It is said Gen Braddock was buried about 8 miles forward from this, near a little brook that crosses the road. Laurel hill is the highest ridge of the Mo. When you get to the top of it to look forward toward Redstone there is a beautiful prospect of the country below the Mo. You see at one view a number of plantations and Beason Town which is six miles off." [55]

With the growth of Cumberland and the improvement of navigation of the upper Potomac, and especially the building of the canal beside it, the importance of the Braddock route across the mountains was realized by the state of Maryland and the legislature passed laws with reference to

[55] Speed's *The Wilderness Road*, p. 60.

straightening and improving it as early as 1795; acts of a similar nature were also passed in 1798 and 1802.[56]

A pilgrim who passed westward with his family over Braddock's Road in 1796 leaves us some interesting details concerning the journey in a letter written from Western Virginia after his arrival in the "Monongahela Country" in the fall of that year. Arriving at Alexandria by boat from Connecticut the party found that it was less expensive and safer to begin land carriage there than to ascend the Potomac further. They then pursued one of the routes of Braddock's army to Cumberland and the Braddock Road from that point to Laurel Hill. The price paid for hauling their goods from Alexandria to Morgantown (now West Virginia) was thirty-two shillings and sixpence per hundred-weight "of women and goods (freight)" — the men "all walked the whole of the way." Crossing "the blue Mountain the Monongehaly & the Lorral Mountains we found the roads to be verry bad."

It is difficult to say when Braddock's

[56] Lowdermilk's *History of Cumberland*, p. 275.

Road, as a route, ceased to be used since portions of it have never been deserted. There are interesting references to it in the records of Allegheny County, Maryland., which bear the dates 1807 [57] and 1813 [58]. A little later it is plain that " Jesse Tomlinson's " is described " on *National Road* " rather than on " *Braddock's Road*," as in 1807. [59] From this it would seem that by 1817 the term " Braddock's Road " was ignored, at least at points where the Cumberland Road had been built upon the old-time track. Elsewhere Braddock's route kept its ancient name and, perhaps, will never exchange it for another.

The rough track of this first highway westward may be followed today almost at any point in all its course between the Potomac and the Monongahela, and the great caverns and gullies which mark so plainly its tortuous course speak as no words can of the sufferings and dangers of those who travelled it during the dark half

[57] *Land Records of Allegheny County, Md.* Liber E, fol. 191.

[58] *Id.*, Liber G, fol. 251.

[59] *Id.*, Liber I and J, fol. 105.

BRADDOCK'S ROAD
IN THE WOODS NEAR FARMINGTON, PENNSYLVANIA

century when it offered one of the few
passage-ways to the West. It was a clear,
sweet October day when I first came into
Great Meadows to make there my home
until those historic hills and plains became
thoroughly familiar to me. From the
Cumberland Road, as one looks southward
from Mount Washington across Great
Meadows and the site of Fort Necessity,
the hillside beyond is well-timbered on the
right and on the left; but between the
forests lies a large tract of cultivated
ground across which runs, in a straight
line, the dark outline of a heavy unhealed
wound. A hundred and fifty years of rain
and snow and frost have been unable to
remove, even from a sloping surface, this
heavy finger mark. Many years of cultivation have not destroyed it, and for many
years yet the plow will jolt and swing
heavily when it crosses the track of Braddock's Road. I was astonished to find that
at many points in Fayette and neighboring
counties the old course of the road can be
distinctly traced in fields which have for
half a century and more been under constant cultivation. If, at certain points,

cultivation and the elements have pounded the old track level with the surrounding ground, a few steps in either direction will bring the explorer instantly to plain evidence of its course — except where the road-bed is, today, a travelled lane or road. On the open hillsides the track takes often the appearance of a terrace, where, in the old days the road tore a great hole along the slope, and formed a catchwater which rendered it a veritable bog in many places. Now and then on level ground the course is marked by a slight rounding hollow which remains damp when the surrounding ground is wet, or is baked very hard when the usual supply of water is exhausted. In some places this strange groove may be seen extending as far as eye can reach, as though it were the pathway of a gigantic serpent across the wold. At times the track, passing the level, meets a slight ridge which, if it runs parallel to its course, it mounts; if the rising ground is encountered at right angles, the road ploughs a gulley straight through, in which the water runs after each rain, preserving the depression once made by the road. And as I journeyed to and fro in that valley visiting the classic spots which appear in such tender grace in the glad sunshine of a mountain autumn, I never passed a spot of open where this old roadway was to be seen without a thrill; as James Lane Allen has so beautifully said of Boone's old road through Cumberland Gap to Kentucky, so may the explorer feelingly exclaim concerning Braddock's old track: "It is impossible to come upon this road without pausing, or to write of it without a tribute."

This is particularly true of Braddock's Road when you find it in the forests; everything that savage mark tells in the open country is reëchoed in mightier tones within the shadows of the woods. There the wide strange track is like nothing of which you ever heard or read. It looks nothing like a roadway. It is plainly not the track of a tornado, though its width and straight course in certain places would suggest this. Yet it is never the same in two places; here, it is a wide straight aisle covered with rank weeds in the center of the low, wet course; there, the forests impinge upon it where the ground is drier;

here, it appears like the abandoned bed of a brook, the large stones removed from its track lying on each side as though strewn there by a river's torrent; there, it swings quickly at right angles near the open where the whole width is covered with velvet grass radiant in the sunshine which can reach it here. In the forests more than elsewhere the deep furrow of the roadway has remained wet, and for this reason trees have not come up. At many points the road ran into marshy ground and here a large number of roundabout courses speak of the desperate struggles the old teamsters had on this early track a century ago. And now and then as you pass along, scattered blocks and remnants of stone chimneys mark the sites of ancient taverns and homesteads.

In the forests it is easy to conjure up the scene when this old track was opened — for it was cut through a " wooden country," to use an expression common among the pioneers. Here you can see the long line of sorry wagons standing in the road when the army is encamped; and though many of them seem unable to carry their loads one

foot further — yet there is ever the ringing
chorus of the axes of six hundred choppers
sounding through the twilight of the hot
May evening. It is almost suffocating in
the forests when the wind does not blow,
and the army is unused to the scorching
American summer which has come early
this year. The wagon train is very long,
and though the van may have halted on
level ground, the line behind stretches
down and up the shadowy ravines. The
wagons are blocked in all conceivable posi-
tions on the hillsides. The condition of
the horses is pitiful beyond description.
If some are near to the brook or spring,
others are far away. Some horses will
never find water tonight. To the right
and left the sentinels are lost in the surrounding gloom.

And then with those singing axes for
the perpetual refrain, consider the mighty
epic poem to be woven out of the days that
have succeeded Braddock here. Though
lost in the Alleghenies, this road and all
its busy days mirror perfectly the social
advance of the western empire to which it
led. Its first mission was to bind, as with

a strange, rough, straggling cincture the
East and the West. The young colonies
were being confined to the Atlantic Ocean
by a chain of forts the French were forging
from Quebec to New Orleans. Had they
not awakened to the task of shattering that
chain it is doubtful if the expansion of the
colonies could ever have meant what it has
to the western world. Could Virginia
have borne a son in the western wilderness,
Kentucky by name, if France had held the
Ohio Valley? Could North Carolina have
given birth to a Tennessee if France had
made good her claim to the Mississippi?
Could New England and New York and
Pennsylvania have produced the fruits the
nineteenth century saw blossom in the Old
Northwest if France had maintained her
hold within that mighty empire? The
rough track of Braddock's Road, almost
forgotten and almost obliterated, is one of
the best memorials of the earliest struggle
of the Colonies for the freedom which was
indispensable to their progress. There
was not an hour throughout the Revolutionary struggle when the knowledge of
the great West that was to be theirs was

not a powerful inspiration to the bleeding colonies; aye, there was not a moment when the gallant commander of those ragged armies forgot that there was a West into which he could retreat at the darkest hour over Braddock's twelve-foot road.

That is the great significance of this first track through the " wooden country " — an awakened consciousness.

The traveller at Uniontown, Pennsylvania, is within striking distance of Braddock's Road at its most interesting points. A six-mile climb to the summit of Laurel Hill brings one upon the old-time route which will be found near Washington's Spring. A delightful drive along the summit of the mountain northward brings one near the notorious " Dunbar's Camp " where so many relics of the campaign have been found and of which many may be seen in the museum of the nearby Pennsylvania Soldiers' Orphans' Home. Here Dunbar destroyed the quantities of stores and ammunition with which he could not advance, much less retreat. The visitor here should find " Jumonville's Grove," about a quarter of a mile up the valley, and should not miss the view from Dunbar's Knob.

Less than one mile eastward of Chalk Hill, beside a brook which bears Braddock's name, beneath a cluster of solemn pines, lies the dust of the sacrificed Braddock. If there is any question as to whether his body was interred at this spot, there is no question but that all the good he ever did is buried here. Deserted by those who should have helped him most, fed with promises that were never kept, defeated because he could not find the breath to cry " retreat " until a French bullet drove it to his throat — he is remembered by his private vices which the whole world would quickly have forgotten had he won his last fight. He was typical of his time — not worse.

In studying Braddock's letters, preserved in the Public Records Office, London, it has been of interest to note that he never blamed an inferior — as he boasted in the anecdote previously related. His most bitter letter has been reproduced, and a study of it will make each line of more interest. His criticism of the Colonial

troops was sharp, but his praise of them
when they had been tried in fire was un-
bounded. He does not directly criticise
St. Clair — though his successful rival for
honors on the Ohio, Forbes, accused St.
Clair in 1758 not only of ignorance but of
actual treachery. "This Behavior in the
people" is Braddock's charge, and no one
will say the accusation was unjust.

With something more than ordinary
good judgment Braddock singled out good
friends. What men in America, at the
time, were more influential in their spheres
than Franklin, Washington, and Morris?
These were almost the only men he, finally,
had any confidence in or respect for.
Washington knew Braddock as well as any
man, and who but Washington, in the happier days of 1784, searched for his grave
by Braddock's Run in vain, desirous of
erecting a monument over it?

Mr. King, editor of the Pittsburg *Com-
mercial-Gazette*, in 1872 took an interest in
Braddock's Grave, planted the pines over
it and enclosed them. A slip from a willow
tree that grew beside Napoleon's grave at
St. Helena was planted here but did not

grow. There is little doubt that Braddock's dust lies here. He was buried in the roadway near this brook, and at this point, early in the last century, workmen repairing the road discovered the remains of an officer. The remains were reinterred here on the high ground beside the Cumberland Road, on the opposite bank of Braddock's Run. They were undoubtedly Braddock's.

As you look westward along the roadway toward the grave, the significant gorge on the right will attract your attention. It is the old pathway of Braddock's Road, the only monument or significant token in the world of the man from whom it was named. Buried once in it — near the cluster of gnarled apple-trees in the center of the open meadow beyond — he is now buried, and finally no doubt, beside it. But its hundreds of great gorges and vacant swampy isles in the forests will last long after any monument that can be raised to his memory.

Braddock's Road broke the league the French had made with the Alleghenies; it showed that British grit could do as much in the interior of America as in India or Africa or Egypt; it was the first important material structure in this New West, so soon to be filled with the sons of those who had hewn it.